50 WALKS IN
Surrey

50 Walks in Surrey

Published by AA Publishing (a trading name of AA Media Limited, whose registered office is Grove House, Lutyens Close, Lychpit, Basingstoke, Hampshire RG24 8AG; registered number 06112600)

© AA Media Limited 2019
First published 2001
Second edition 2008
Third edition 2014
This edition 2019, reprinted 2021

Field checked and updated by Richard Marchi.

Mapping in this book is derived from the following products:
OS Landranger 175 (walks 34-36, 43, 47)
OS Landranger 176 (walks 24-25, 33)
OS Landranger 186 (walks 29-32, 38-42, 44-46, 48-50)
OS Landranger 187 (walks 1-23, 26-28)
OS Explorer 145 (walk 37)

© Crown copyright and database rights 2016 Ordnance Survey. 100021153.

A CIP catalogue record for this book is available from the British Library.

ISBN: 978-0-7495-8123-7
ISBN (SS): 978-0-7495-7585-4

Series management: Clare Ashton
Editor: Rebecca Fry
Designer: Tom Whitlock
Digital imaging & repro: Ian Little
Cartography provided by the Mapping Services Department of AA Publishing.

Printed and bound in the UK by Bell & Bain Ltd, Glasgow

A05792

We would like to thank the following photographers, companies and picture libraries for their assistance in the preparation of this book. Abbreviations for the picture credits are as follows:
Alamy = Alamy Stock Photo
12/13 Tony Peacock/Alamy; 23 Greg Balfour Evans/Alamy; 39 Keith Heron/Alamy; 49 Tomas Burian/Alamy; 71 Julia Gavin/Alamy; 93 Greg Balfour Evans/Alamy; 109 Louise Heusinkveld/Alamy; 122-123 Mark Kerrison/Alamy; 149 PETER HUGGINS/Alamy; 160-169 Denis Chapman/Alamy

The contents of this book are believed correct at the time of printing. Nevertheless, the publishers cannot be held responsible for any errors or omissions or for changes in the details given in this book or for the consequences of any reliance on the information it provides. This does not affect your statutory rights. We have tried to ensure accuracy in this book, but things do change and we would be grateful if readers would advise us of any inaccuracies they may encounter by emailing walks@aamediagroup.co.uk

We have done our best to make sure that these walks are safe and achievable by walkers with a basic level of fitness. However, we can accept no responsibility for any loss or injury incurred while following the walks. Advice on walking safely can be found on pages 10–11.

Some of the walks may appear in other AA books and publications.

Discover and book AA-rated places to stay at RatedTrips.com

AA

50 WALKS IN
Surrey

CONTENTS

The walks

HOW TO USE THIS BOOK

Each walk starts with an information panel giving all the information you will need about the walk at a glance, including its relative difficulty, distance and total amount of ascent. Difficulty levels and gradients are as follows:

Difficulty of walk

● Easy

● Intermediate

● Hard

Gradient

▲ Some slopes

▲▲ Some steep slopes

▲▲▲ Several very steep slopes

Maps

Every walk has its own route map. We also suggest a relevant AA or Ordnance Survey map to take with you, allowing you to view the area in more detail. The time suggested is the minimum for reasonably fit walkers and doesn't allow for stops.

Route map legend

––––▸––	Walk route	▦	Built-up area
❶	Route waypoint	▢	Woodland area
– – – –	Adjoining path	🚻	Toilet
•	Place of interest	P	Car park
⌂	Steep section	⌷	Picnic area
⧵ⅼ⁄	Viewpoint	)(	Bridge

Start points

The start of each walk is given as a six-figure grid reference prefixed by two letters referring to a 100km square of the National Grid. More information on grid references can be found on most OS and AA Walker's Maps.

Dogs

We have tried to give dog owners useful advice about how dog friendly each walk is. Please respect other countryside users. Keep your dog under control, especially around livestock, and obey local bylaws and other dog control notices.

Car parking

Many of the car parks suggested are public, but occasionally you may have to park on the roadside or in a lay-by. Please be considerate about where you leave your car, ensuring that you are not on private property or access roads, and that gates are not blocked and other vehicles can pass safely.

Walks locator map

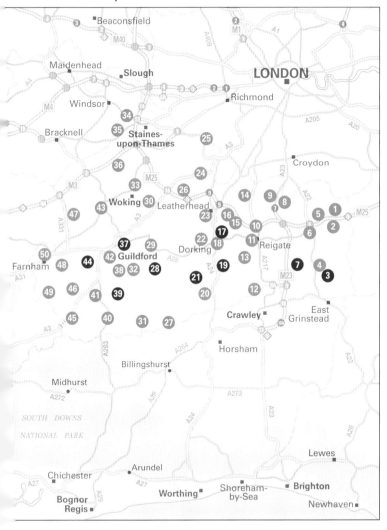

EXPLORING THE AREA

Best known as the ultimate commuter-belt county, affluent, well-manicured Surrey, in England's southeast, nevertheless has some wonderful walking country to its name. Bordered by Greater London to the north, Kent to the west, Hampshire and Sussex to the south and Berkshire to the west, Surrey's boundaries have changed quite a bit over the years, particularly in the 19th and 20th century, when they once stretched as far into London as Wandsworth. These days it is still sometimes difficult to know where Greater London ends and Surrey begins.

There's not much evidence still in existence of the county's ancient inhabitants, although two interesting examples of Bronze Age barrows or burial mounds survive at Woking's Horsell Common and the remains of Iron Age hillforts can be seen at Hascombe Hill, Chertsey, and St George's Hill in Weybridge. The hillfort at Holmbury Hill is a great destination for walkers as a yomp up to the site rewards them with breathtaking views of the surrounding countryside.

The Saxons arrived in Surrey in the 5th and 6th centuries and their tribal names still resonate in modern placenames such as Woking and Godalming. The name 'Surrey' itself comes from the Saxon word *Suthrige*, meaning southern kingdom.

Surrey may be better known for its suburbia than its scenery, but the image is unjust. Over a quarter of the county's landscapes are official Areas of Outstanding Natural Beauty, and along the downs and the greensand ridge you can gaze across to distant horizons with hardly a building in sight. Surprisingly, perhaps, this is one of England's most wooded counties, and it has more village greens than any other shire. You'll find sandy tracks and cottage gardens, folded hillsides and welcoming village inns. There's variety, too, as the fields and meadows of the east give way to the wooded downs and valleys west of the River Mole.Of course there are also large built-up areas, mainly within and around the M25; but even here you can still find some appealing walks. On the fringe of Greater London you can picnic in Chaldon's hay meadows, explore the wide open downs at Epsom, or drift idly beside the broad reaches of the stately River Thames.

Deep in the Surrey countryside you'll discover remnants of the Romans at Farley Heath, and mingle with the monks at England's first Cistercian monastery. You'll see buildings by great architects like Edwin Lutyens and Sir George Gilbert Scott, and meet authors too, from John Donne to Agatha Christie. Then, among a host of curiosities, you'll unearth London's lost route to the sea, and find out how information technology put Chatley on line fully 15 years before Queen Victoria ascended the throne.

Six long-distance routes, including two National Trails, weave their way around the county, and you'll get the chance to sample sections of all of them as you journey through these pages. The Thames Path needs no introduction on its royal progress from Runnymede to Hampton Court. Next comes the North Downs Way, linking Farnham with Canterbury and Dover; a little further south, the Greensand Way runs east along the glorious ridge from Haslemere to Oxted. The Downs Link and the Wey South Path follow disused and delightfully flat rail and canal routes south from Guildford, connecting Surrey with the glorious South Downs Way. Finally, the Sussex Border Path slips in and out of the county between Haslemere and East Grinstead as it tracks the boundary with Surrey's southern neighbour.

So pull on your walking boots, dig out the maps, and set out on Surrey's magnificent highways and byways.

PUBLIC TRANSPORT

For details of public transport services in Surrey, see travelsmartsurrey.info/public-transport, where there are links to the National Rail Enquiries website and timetables for bus routes in and about the county.

WALKING IN SAFETY

All these walks are suitable for any reasonably fit person, but less experienced walkers should try the easier walks first. Route-finding is usually straightforward, but you will find that an Ordnance Survey or AA walking map is a useful addition to the route maps and descriptions; recommendations can be found in the information panels.

Risks

Although each walk here has been researched with a view to minimising the risks to the walkers who follow its route, no walk in the countryside can be considered to be completely free from risk. Walking in the outdoors will always require a degree of common sense and judgement to ensure that it is as safe as possible.

- Be particularly careful on cliff paths and in upland terrain, where the consequences of a slip can be very serious.

- Remember to check tidal conditions before walking on the seashore.

- Some sections of route are by, or cross, busy roads. Take care, and remember that traffic is a danger even on minor country lanes.

- Be careful around farmyard machinery and livestock, especially if you have children with you.

- Be aware of the consequences of changes in the weather, and check the forecast before you set out. Carry spare clothing and a torch if you are walking in the winter months. Remember that the weather can change very quickly at any time of the year, and in moorland and heathland areas, mist and fog can make route-finding much harder. Don't set out in these conditions unless you are confident of your navigation skills in poor visibility.

- In summer remember to take account of the heat and sun; wear a hat and carry water.

- On walks away from centres of population you should carry a whistle and survival bag. If you do have an accident that means you require help from the emergency services, make a note of your position as accurately as possible and dial 999.

Countryside Code
Respect other people:

- Consider the local community and other people enjoying the outdoors.

- Co-operate with people at work in the countryside. For example, keep out of the way when farm animals are being gathered or moved, and follow directions from the farmer.

- Don't block gateways, driveways or other paths with your vehicle.
- Leave gates and property as you find them, and follow paths unless wider access is available, such as on open country or registered common land (known as 'open access land').
- Leave machinery and farm animals alone – don't interfere with animals, even if you think they're in distress. Try to alert the farmer instead.
- Use gates, stiles or gaps in field boundaries if you can – climbing over walls, hedges and fences can damage them and increase the risk of farm animals escaping.
- Our heritage matters to all of us – be careful not to disturb ruins and historic sites.

Protect the natural environment:
- Take your litter home. Litter and leftover food don't just spoil the beauty of the countryside; they can be dangerous to wildlife and farm animals. Dropping litter and dumping rubbish are criminal offences.
- Leave no trace of your visit, and take special care not to damage, destroy or remove features such as rocks, plants and trees.
- Keep dogs under effective control, making sure they are not a danger or nuisance to farm animals, horses, wildlife or other people.
- If cattle or horses chase you and your dog, it is safer to let your dog off the lead – don't risk getting hurt by trying to protect it. Your dog will be much safer if you let it run away from a farm animal in these circumstances, and so will you.
- Everyone knows how unpleasant dog mess is and it can cause infections, so always clean up after your dog and get rid of the mess responsibly – bag it and bin it.
- Fires can be as devastating to wildlife and habitats as they are to people and property – so be careful with naked flames and cigarettes at any time of the year.

Enjoy the outdoors:
- Plan ahead and be prepared for natural hazards, changes in weather and other events.
- Wild animals, farm animals and horses can behave unpredictably if you get too close, especially if they're with their young – so give them plenty of space.
- Follow advice and local signs

For more information visit naturalengland.org.uk/ourwork/enjoying/countrysidecode

WOODLAND WALK FROM TITSEY TO TATSFIELD

DISTANCE/TIME	3.5 miles (5.7km) / 1hr 30min
ASCENT/GRADIENT	531ft (162m) / ▲
PATHS	Woodland on the North Downs Way, then across farmland to Tatsfield village, some roads, 2 stiles
LANDSCAPE	High on the North Downs with good views
SUGGESTED MAP	OS Explorers 146 Dorking, Box Hill & Reigate & 147 Sevenoaks & Tonbridge
START/FINISH	Grid reference: TQ398555
DOG FRIENDLINESS	Good, but some road sections and lead required across farmland
PARKING	Botley Hill Car park, Titsey Foundation
PUBLIC TOILETS	None on route

Notice boards in the car park at Botley Hill provide information about Titsey Place, which lies in the valley below. It is an estate with a rich history, and it has been well maintained to make it a fascinating place to visit. Its origins go back to the 16th century, when it was bought by Sir John Gresham, a Lord Mayor of London and a prominent merchant who initiated trade with Russia that led to an agreement signed by Queen Elizabeth I and Ivan the Terrible.

Manor of Titsey

Gresham became very wealthy, and bought the Manor of Titsey from the Crown. He built a large house, only a small portion of which survives today. Although he did not live at the house, Sir John's nephew, Thomas, would become one of the most influential people in Elizabethan England. He was Chancellor to the Queen and he built the Royal Exchange in London.

The family (and the house) suffered during the Civil War and the house became completely dilapidated during the 18th century. The family built a smaller house on the site, which was enlarged to its present size during the 19th century. The Greshams married well and acquired great wealth and political power, and the estate was improved and expanded with the building of St James's Church in Titsey, the modifications in the house and the development of the gardens. This wealthy family has filled the house with a multitude of treasures from furniture and porcelain to masterpieces, including four by Canaletto and portraits by Reynolds, Romney and Lely.

The gardens are equally spectacular: the lake at the heart of the gardens carries the stream that encouraged the early residents of Titsey to stay there. It is only a small stream at this point, but it goes on to flow into the River Medway. The cascade, the fountain and the lakes bring a romantic atmosphere, and support a wide variety of wildlife. The rest of the gardens are a delight. The Kitchen Garden was restored to recreate the style of a Victorian garden in 1996, with glasshouses, hedging and paths, and fruit of all kinds is grown there. The Rose Garden was redesigned and replanted in 2002. One of the latest additions to the estate is the Tea Room, which is housed in the refurbished dairy buildings of Home Farm. On the hill above the house are two blocks of woodland with well-marked trails that provide superb views across the estate. Some of the paths are very steep, but they make for good exercise.

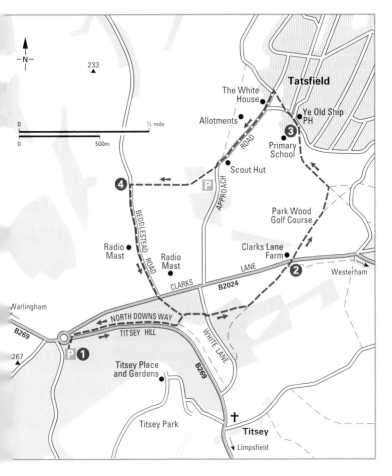

1. From the car park, walk to the road and turn right along Titsey Hill to a road crossing in 35yds (32m). Turn left across the road to a fingerpost and follow the North Downs Way (NDW). After 750yds (686m), at a waymarker, turn left up steps and, at the next waymarker at the top of the slope, bear right on the NDW and continue to White Lane. Turn right down the road, then immediately left along the NDW through woodland. At the edge of the wood, go up five wooden steps to a kissing gate and across the field. Head towards woodland to pass through a kissing gate and follow the path, which eventually meets a road (Clarks Lane). Cross with care to a fingerpost diagonally right.

2. Go over a stile beside a gate into the field and walk half right across the field, in part alongside a barbed wire fence. Cross a stile and follow the public

footpath across part of Park Wood Golf Course. Continue across the course on the waymarked grassy public footpath as it bears half left, heading for the furthest row of conifers. Go through a gap in the trees and turn left. This path follows the side of a field and eventually descends down steps to a track. Cross the track, go through two gates and head uphill to another gate. Continue ahead to pass Tatsfield Primary School to reach a kissing gate. Go through this to the road, and turn left and continue to Tatsfield village.

3. Pass the Ye Old Ship Inn, then cross the road and walk across the middle of Westmore Green on the path, turn left on Lusted Hall Lane and pass The White House, continue into Approach Road and walk along the grassy verge on the left side of it. Continue for 475yds (434m) and, just past the Scout Hut on the left, reach Furze Corner with a playing field sign. Cross the road and turn left, then, just before the car park, turn right along the public footpath indicated by the waymarker. The narrow path emerges into a field. Continue across the field and descend to a kissing gate hidden in the hedge.

4. Turn left along Beddlestead Road and continue to Clarks Lane. Jink left then cross the road and go down the public footpath at the fingerpost to reach the NDW. Bear right and descend steeply to a flight of steps, then turn right at the bottom and continue to Titsey Hill road. Cross with care, turn right and return to the car park.

Where to eat and drink

There is a good pub, Ye Old Ship, in Tatsfield, about halfway round the walk. It is friendly and provides a good range of reasonably priced food. It has a spacious garden for those fine days.

What to see

Close to the car park you'll find Titsey Place and Gardens, which lie in the valley below it. They are open from mid-May to September, Wednesdays and weekends (visit www.titsey.org for details), and the Tea Room serves light lunches and refreshments. Access to the woodlands above the house is free and open most of the year, and they make an energetic extension to this walk or a fresh excursion.

OXTED AND THE NORTH DOWNS WAY

DISTANCE/TIME	5.8 miles (9.3km) / 2hrs 45min
ASCENT/GRADIENT	938ft (286m) / ▲ ▲ ▲
PATHS	Field edge paths, farm tracks, town roads, 6 stiles
LANDSCAPE	Townscape, downland and chalk cliffs – keep well back from the cliff edges
SUGGESTED MAP	OS Explorer 146 Dorking, Box Hill & Reigate
START/FINISH	Grid reference: TQ395529
DOG FRIENDLINESS	Good on Downs, around Oxted dogs must be on leads
PARKING	Ellice Road car park, off Station Road East, Oxted. ANPR, charges apply Monday-Friday 8am-5pm
PUBLIC TOILETS	At car park

If Swindon or Crewe is your idea of a railway town, then you're in for a surprise. The railway came late to the medieval village of Oxted – just how late, we'll see in a moment – but it didn't destroy the character of the place. Instead, when Oxted expanded to embrace the new arrival, it developed its own unique style. To begin with, it looked as if Oxted wouldn't get a railway at all. Parliament had authorised an independent line between Croydon and Royal Tunbridge Wells in 1865 but, in all but name, it was part of a turf war between two powerful companies competing for traffic between London and Hastings.

Parts of the line were actually built, including the tunnel on the walk. But there were all kinds of difficulties, including a riot against the contractor's Belgian workforce, and work was abandoned around 1870. Years passed, and in 1878 Parliament approved new proposals for a railway linking Croydon, Oxted and East Grinstead. This time the old rivals were working in partnership. The new scheme took over the abandoned works from the 1860s, and construction went ahead smoothly. After a wait of almost 20 years, the line through Oxted finally opened in March 1884.

By coincidence, the Fabian Society of socialist thinkers was formed in the same year. One of its founder members was Edward Pease, who lived at nearby Limpsfield. He and others soon discovered that they could live in the country without having to cut themselves off from London society. Intellectuals such as D H Lawrence, George Bernard Shaw and Sidney and Beatrice Webb were among many who used the railway to attend Fabian gatherings. The author Hilaire Belloc also used the railway – though he didn't come by train. In his book *The Old Road*, Belloc describes how he set out to prove the route of the Pilgrim's Way by walking the track from Winchester to Canterbury himself. He reached the cutting near Oxted tunnel at nightfall, and stumbled down the railway line in search of an inn.

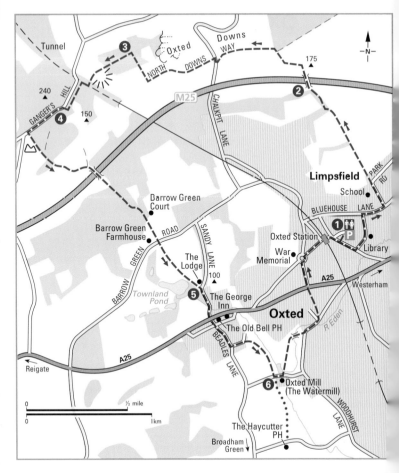

1. Take the walkway from the corner of the car park (by the toilets) to Station Road East and turn left. Turn left again when you get to Gresham Road, then turn right at the top into Bluehouse Lane. Lastly, turn left again into Park Road and, at the bend, continue straight ahead on the signposted public footpath towards Woldingham, between the school and its playing fields. Cross the stile beyond the playing fields, and head around the field edge towards the footbridge over the M25 motorway.

2. Cross the motorway, and follow the path to the left to go through a metal kissing gate and swing left onto the North Downs Way (NDW). Follow this breezy downland path to reach a signposted T-junction, and bear left on the NDW to drop down steeply, through a kissing gate to a lane. Turn right for 30yds (27m) and then left, signed NDW. Soon pass through a kissing gate and follow the field edge until it turns right for the assault on the North Downs ridge. Pass through another two kissing gates before bearing left.

3. Follow the path as it burrows through the trees, and turn hard right up a flight of 110 steps. Don't miss the view from the seat a third of the way up, directly above the railway tunnel. Swing left at the top of the steps, and

follow the NDW to the road at Ganger's Hill. On reaching a few more steps on your right continue ahead on the NDW.

4. Continue on the path below the road until reaching a fingerpost, then turn left off the NDW, dropping down towards Oxted. Join the bridleway halfway down, and carry on across the bridge over the M25 onto the lane past Barrow Green Court on your left. Cross over Barrow Green Road, squeeze through the kissing gate buried in the hedge directly opposite, then follow the fenced footpath along the edge of the field past Townland Pond, on your right, and out onto Sandy Lane, beside The Lodge.

5. Turn right, pass underneath the A25, and cross Oxted High Street at The Old Bell pub. Follow Beadles Lane for 200yds (183m), then turn left into Springfield and fork off onto a footpath at the bend in the road. Drop gently down to Spring Lane, and the picturesque Oxted Mill (The Watermill is privately owned). (A 500yd (457m) diversion, on the Greensand Way, leads you to The Haycutter pub, crossing straight over Spring Lane. Zig-zag right and left, then take the waymarked path through a kissing gate, over three stiles and through the meadows to the pub.)

6. The main route turns left past the mill, and left again over the stile at the sluice gate. Follow the path over a stile and a little bridge through to Woodhurst Lane, and turn left. Turn left again into Woodhurst Park and take the narrow footpath on the right, and cross the A25 into East Hill Road. At the foot of the hill, turn right up Station Road West, then go through the station subway at the top. Turn right into Station Road East to return to the car park.

Where to eat and drink

On the High Street in Old Oxted, The Old Bell is a Chef and Brewer pub with a heavily beamed Tudor interior. They also serve meals in a bar area. Nearby on the High Street is The George Inn, a Grade II listed former coaching inn with a relaxed atmosphere and an excellent restaurant, which serves real ales and bar meals. In Broadham Green, The Haycutter is an unpretentious country pub, popular with locals. The traditional food is worth waiting for. There's a garden and they serve real ales.

What to see

As the area's popularity grew, the railway became the natural focus for expansion. From the dawn of the 20th century through to the 1930s, the Williams family of local builders developed the 'Oxted Mock Tudor' style to blend the new town with the genuine half-timbered Tudor buildings of Old Oxted. The National Westminster Bank in Station Road East is a good example, but another favourite is the Everyman cinema in Station Road West. You'll pass them both, near the start and finish of the walk, and you can compare them with the real thing on your way up through Old Oxted.

While you're there

Winston Churchill's home at Chartwell, to the south of Westerham, is a country house set in delightful gardens, and contains many mementos of his illustrious career. It's owned by the National Trust, and there are the usual tea room and gift shop as well as excellent facilities for children.

LINGFIELD TO HAXTED MILL

DISTANCE/TIME	6.3 miles (10.1km) / 2hrs 30min
ASCENT/GRADIENT	220ft (67m) / ▲
PATHS	Field edge paths can be overgrown or muddy, farm tracks and country lanes, 15 stiles
LANDSCAPE	Flattish farmland in headwaters of the River Eden
SUGGESTED MAP	OS Explorers 146 Dorking, Box Hill & Reigate & 147 Sevenoaks and Tonbridge
START/FINISH	Grid reference: TQ385435
DOG FRIENDLINESS	Poor; lead needed around farmyards, livestock and traffic, and numerous stiles may prove troublesome
PARKING	Council car park in Gun Pit Road, Lingfield (free for 3 hours then pay and display)
PUBLIC TOILETS	None on route

Out on the Surrey border, the charming little Starborough Castle was home to one of the grandest families in the land. The Cobham family had lived at Starborough since at least the 14th century, and Reginald, the first Lord Cobham, also owned nearby Hever Castle. Lord Cobham held office as Admiral of the Fleet and Lord Warden of the Cinque Ports, he fought at Crecy with the Black Prince, and was among the first of the Knights of the Garter.

Decline and fall
Ironically, Lord Cobham survived his distinguished military career only to die of the plague in 1361. In his will, the great man left Haxted Mill to his wife, Joan. It was a more enduring legacy than the family home because, in a further twist of fate, Parliament ordered the demolition of Starborough Castle at the end of the Civil War. More than a century later the site was remodelled by Sir James Burrow, who used medieval materials to build the present Gothic-style pavilion. His building was restored during the 1980s, and is now a private home.

The daily grind
By contrast, the mill that you'll see at Point 4 on this walk still stands on its original foundations at Haxted. According to local tradition, Haxted Mill was founded by Richard III in the 15th century, though the earlier half of the present building was constructed on 14th-century foundations around 1580. The builders used local hand-axed oak to build the mill, and a sawn pitch pine extension was added in 1794. Haxted Mill continued grinding flour until just after World War I, when it switched to producing meal for the local farmers. Milling ended in 1945, and it has been both a museum and an upmarket restaurant, but is now closed with an uncertain future.

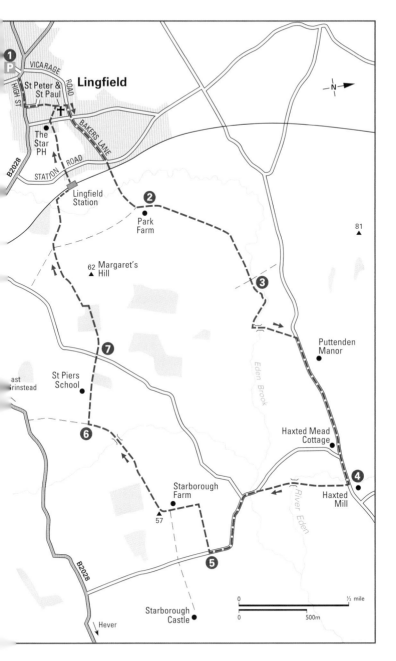

1. From the car park, cross East Grinstead Road and continue down the High Street. Turn left into Old School Place, and take the footpath between houses through the churchyard. Turn right into Vicarage Road, cross into Bakers Lane, and continue beyond Station Road, jink left and then right onto the footpath across the railway. Swing left as you approach Park Farm, then fork left onto

a gravelled farm track, following the public footpath signs, in front of a row of houses and then ahead on a grassy track.

2. Continue over the stile into a field. After a few paces, cross a concrete bridge and then the stile on your left, and continue with the hedge on your right. At the field top corner, turn right through the kissing gate, heading diagonally across the field, past the prominent oak tree, towards the gate and adjoining stile on the far side of the field.

3. Cross the lane, climb over the stile opposite, and follow the footpath beside Eden Brook. Cross the brook on a new black metal bridge, then head across the field to a stile by the metal gates. Turn right along the road to Haxted Mill.

4. Cross the stile and turn right onto the Vanguard Way, re-cross the river, and bear left towards the stile on the far side of the next field. Turn left onto the road, then fork left just beyond the bridge.

5. Turn right along the drive towards Starborough Farm. At the farm, take the stile on the left, just before the wooden gates leading to the house. Walk along the field edge and then between farm buildings to reach a stile in the tree hedge. Cross the drive to Badger House, bear right leaving the house on your right, and follow the path across the field to the corner of a wood. Cross the footbridge and pass through a gate into a field and follow its left-hand edge ahead, then continue following the left-hand field edge to cross the next three fields, with either a stile or gate between each field.

6. Turn right in the corner of the fourth field, keeping the hedge on your left, and continue over a bridge and stile and follow the field edge on your left, over another bridge and stile into St Piers School sports ground. Keeping the hedge on your right, continue to a gap just before the corner of the hedge ahead, then cross the lane, where the footpath continues at a stile.

7. Cross a small field, a footbridge and then a second field, exiting via a stile. A few paces on, enter the woods by a gate, and pass the school's adventure playground. Beyond the woods, bear right through the gates near the school buildings, and follow the left-hand edge of the field. In a second field, jink left onto a path to pass close to sports pitches. Pass through a kissing gate, and over two footbridges separated by a meadow to reach the railway line. Turn right and cross the line over the footbridge in the station. Walk down the approach road to cross over Station Road and up the path opposite The Star Inn. Cross over Church Road, and turn right through the charming Old Town into the churchyard. Finally, retrace your steps to the car park.

Where to eat and drink

In Lingfield, The Star is a large pub with real ales and food served all day at the weekends, lunch and dinner Monday to Friday. Children are welcome up to 9pm, and dogs are allowed in the bar.

What to see

After seeing the mill, drop in on Lord Cobham and his relations. His tomb is among the family memorials in Lingfield Church, and his effigy lies in full plate armour, with his head resting on a Moorish helmet.

FROM BLINDLEY HEATH VIA CROWHURST PLACE

DISTANCE/TIME	5.1 miles (8.2km) / 2hrs 30min
ASCENT/GRADIENT	194ft (59m) / ▲
PATHS	Farm tracks and well-maintained field paths, some road walking, 10 stiles
LANDSCAPE	Gentle, well-farmed landscape
SUGGESTED MAP	OS Explorer 146 Dorking, Box Hill & Reigate
START/FINISH	Grid reference: TQ364453
DOG FRIENDLINESS	Lead required along roads, through farmyards and near livestock; large dogs may have difficulty with stiles
PARKING	Adjoining cricket field on Ray Lane, Blindley Heath
PUBLIC TOILETS	None on route

Nowadays, Crowhurst is on the way to nowhere at all, but apparently things were different in the 16th century. According to tradition, Henry VIII would stop over at Crowhurst Place on his way to court Anne Boleyn, who was living just over the Kentish border at Hever Castle. Even then, Crowhurst Place was not new. The lovely timbered and moated manor may be a spectacular example of what most of us loosely call 'Tudor', but it was already half a century old when that dynasty was ushered in on Bosworth Field in 1485.

The Gaynesford family first pops up during Edward III's reign, when John and Margery Gaynesford received the Manor of Crowhurst from the de Stangrave family. But it was another John Gaynesford – the Sheriff of Surrey, no less – whose dogged pursuit of an heir was to bring him an unbroken run of 15 daughters from his first five wives, eventually fathering a son by his sixth wife. The Gaynesford (later Gainsford) family lasted some 300 years at Crowhurst Place, and it's worth the short diversion to see their tombs, flanking the chancel of Crowhurst's medieval church. There's also a 15th-century brass likeness of John Gaynesford, Surrey's Parliamentary representative in 1431.

Two hundred years later, one of John's descendants left an altogether different memorial of his own. We know from the 17th-century parish register that, in those days, it was 'a loathsom durtie way every steppe' from Crowhurst Place to the church. Tiring of these muddy pilgrimages, yet another John Gainsford paid £50 to have a stone-flagged causeway laid along the entire route. He got his money's worth, for the causeway still exists today in places.

By the dawn of the 20th century, Crowhurst Place was bearded with brambles, lonely and unloved. Its saviour was George Crawley, whose comprehensive restoration in 1920 even extended to the brand new mock-Tudor gatehouse on Crowhurst Road. Crowhurst Place isn't open to the public, but you'll see Crawley's handiwork clearly enough from the path, which runs within 100yds (91m) of the house.

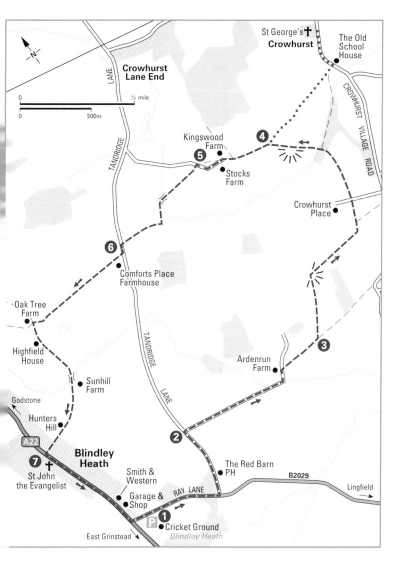

1. Turn right out of the car park, and follow Ray Lane as far as Tandridge Lane. Turn left, pass The Red Barn pub, then turn right up the tree-lined drive towards Ardenrun Farm.

2. Walk up the long straight drive until it swings to the left. Follow it for a further 80yds (73m) then, just before the private drive to Ardenrun Farm, turn right at a fingerpost on a path beside a metal gate. Continue for another 300yds (274m).

3. Cross the stile on the left and walk along the field boundary, over a second stile and bear half right, following the yellow waymarks, marked 'Age to Age Walk'. At the top, turn right at the next waymark – where there are good views behind you –then cross the stile (yellow waymark) and a third field, keeping the hedge on your left, to go through a kissing gate. Follow the

well-maintained path straight across the drive to Crowhurst Place. Pass through a kissing gate and continue beside the hedge on your right. Cross a concrete footbridge, then head diagonally across the next field to the junction of two tarmac tracks. There are more good views from this spot. (To visit Crowhurst church, turn right for 700yds (640m), then left onto Crowhurst Village Road. The church is on your left.)

4. Turn left here, and follow the track towards Stocks and Kingswood farms. Leave the 'Age to Age' route, and carry straight along the yellow waymarked track that winds through Kingswood farmyard, past some small industrial units on the right, and onto a surfaced lane, with Stocks Farmhouse on your left.

5. After passing through the sliding metal barrier that crosses the drive, continue ahead for 22yds (20m) and cross over two stiles, on the left, in quick succession. Head diagonally across the next field, and turn left over the stile. Cross a wide concrete bridge and turn left to reach another stile, in a hedge, and a small footbridge. Now turn right, past a broken stile and hug the right-hand side of the next field to another stile, again follow the right-hand side of the field and leave via a stile onto Tandridge Lane.

6. Turn left and, after 55yds (50m), branch off to the right at the entrance to Comforts Place Farmhouse. As the drive swings round to the left, go through a gap beside a large metal gate and continue along the grassy lane to go through a gap next to a gate and reach a four-way cross tracks at Oak Tree Farm. Turn left here, and follow the rough track past Highfield House, down a narrow path alongside paddocks and out onto a lane. Beyond the gates of Sunhill Farm, the road surface improves, and the lane leads back to the A22.

7. Turn left, and follow the main road for the last 800yds (732m) into Blindley Heath and back to the car park.

Where to eat and drink

You won't go hungry in Blindley Heath, which has two pubs offering extensive all-day menus. Despite its location next to a filling station on the busy A22, the family-friendly Smith & Western Bar, Grill and Diner is set well back from the road in its own gardens. The busy family atmosphere of The Red Barn in Tandridge Lane rather offsets its quieter situation. This popular pub offers a large garden with a children's play area.

What to see

Just a stone's throw from the layby near The Red Barn pub is Blindley Heath Common, a chalk grassland rich in flora and fauna, preserved as a Sight of Special Scientific Interest (SSSI) and managed by Surrey Wildlife Trust. Between mid-April and August you may hear nightingales here.

While you're there

A short drive to the east, just in Kent, you'll find Chiddingstone Castle, a superb historic house with impressive collections of Buddhist and Egyptian artefacts, Japanese armour and Jacobean paintings. There are nature trails in the grounds, as well as a rose garden, fishing lake and Victorian tea room. It's open March to October, Sunday to Wednesday.

WOLDINGHAM AND MARDEN PARK

DISTANCE/TIME	4.2 miles (6.8km) / 2hrs 15min
ASCENT/GRADIENT	761ft (232m) / ▲▲
PATHS	Well-surfaced tracks, some footpaths can become muddy, 1 stile
LANDSCAPE	Superb views at many points both to the north and south
SUGGESTED MAP	OS Explorer 146 Dorking, Box Hill & Reigate
START/FINISH	Grid reference: TQ373541
DOG FRIENDLINESS	Generally very good
PARKING	Marden Park car park, Gangers Hill Road
PUBLIC TOILETS	None on route, the nearest are at the car park on the A22 near Point 3 of the walk

Woldingham, a quiet village that lies just to the north of this walk, was a remote agricultural hamlet until the coming of the railway. There is an early record of a settlement in the Domesday Book, and William the Conqueror gave the parish to one of his knights. The old church, St Agatha's, dates from around 1270, but the present church was built in 1933.

A lavish house

The character of the parkland to the south of Woldingham, Marden Park, was transformed in 1671 when it was acquired by a wealthy moneylender from London, Sir Robert Clayton. He built a lavish house and grounds in the park, which were said to be 'large and well-walled... with innumerable plantations of trees, especially walnuts'. Over the years the house attracted many well-known guests, including Lord Macauley and William Wilberforce. The French emperor, Louis Napoleon, spent most of his exile here. Tragically, this luxurious house burned down in 1879, but the old walled garden, the belfry and the courtyard with its fountain have remained. The house was rebuilt almost straight away in a Victorian style. During World War II, Canadian troops were quartered there, and by 1945 the house was in a state of disrepair. The Society of the Sacred Heart purchased the house, and it is now Woldingham School.

Ancient woodland

The surrounding countryside includes Marden Park Woods, which have been designated as a Site of Special Scientific Interest. The ancient woodland has a great variety of tree species, which produce wonderful colours in autumn. They are home to roe deer, tawny owls and the rare Roman snail. Several types of orchid, striped-wing grasshoppers and around 25 kinds of butterfly can all be found on the chalk grasslands. The woods are owned by the Woodland Trust and this is their largest landholding in Surrey. Great Church Wood was owned for a time by the great conductor Sir Adrian Boult (1889–1983). There is a mine underneath Marden Park (which is around Point

3 of your walk). It dates from the 19th century, and involved the quarrying of firestone and hearthstone. Towards the end of that century it became a mushroom farm, but during World War II it was converted into a secure bonded store and sealed with heavy metal doors. There are still tracks of a railway line inside, but it is now too dangerous to enter.

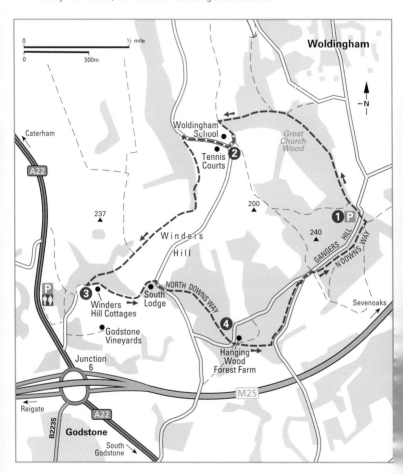

1. From the car park, walk past the wooden gate marked 'Woodland Trust' and take the path straight ahead signed 'Woldingham Countryside Walk' (WCW) on a small marker post. Walk gently downhill and keep ahead passing steps up to your right and down on your left. At the next junction, near a black barn, bear left to follow the sign for Woldingham Station. At the next fingerpost continue ahead, towards South Lodge. At the T-junction opposite a gate and several large green metal containers, turn left, signed to South Lodge, and carry on as the path meets a tarmac drive at the school.

2. Turn right and then right again, passing Marden House on your right and then tennis courts and all weather pitches on the left. The drive starts to bend to the right and, in front of the façade of the old building, turn sharp left at a

fingerpost, back up a hill towards a waymarker. Continue on the well-defined path, slowly climbing up the hillside with a barbed wire fence on the left, and at the top edge of the wood bear right. At the next waymarker, turn left over a stile, and at the far end of the wood the path bears right and ascends between fields. Carry straight on at the next waymarker – on your left the field sweeps down the hillside to the drive leading to South Lodge. Bear left around a thicket and head towards the wood, entering it through an obvious opening. Go into the wood where, after 13yds (12m), another waymarker indicates a path joining from the right. Carry on ahead here and, in 25yds (23m), the path veers to the left and re-enters the field. Continue across this field towards a wood, where the path descends via wooden steps.

3. At the bottom, turn left along the North Downs Way (NDW), passing Winders Hill Cottages and a metal barrier. The path rises gradually with woodland on the left. Cross a chalky track and, on reaching South Lodge on the right, bear right, then sharp left uphill, following the NDW. Pass a seat and continue to follow NDW markers to reach a road and take the few steps down to it.

4. Cross the road by Hanging Wood Forest Farm, and continue along the NDW. As the path descends towards another road, turn left through a kissing gate signed NDW and take the path parallel with the road. Go left up steps and continue alongside the road. Where the path joins the road near a road junction, proceed to the junction and turn right along the road for 85yds (78m), then turn right on the NDW. At a T-junction with a footpath, turn right for 35yds (32m), then left. In 25yds (23m), reach a seat, a notice board and wonderful views. Ignoring a path to the right, continue ahead and then, as the NDW turns to the right at a fingerpost, go left up a flight of steps to the road. Cross the road to return to the car park.

Where to eat and drink

At Point 3, take a detour to visit the Godstone Vineyards. The route takes you down Quarry Road for 500yds (457m) to the entrance to the vineyard. There is a café serving light refreshments, and a shop where their products are for sale (check www.godstonevineyards.com for opening times and more information).

What to see

Woldingham School lies on a part of this walk. An independent girls school, it is run by the Roman Catholic Society of the Sacred Heart, and is set in beautiful grounds.

While you're there

On the north side of Caterham is Kenley Aerodrome, one of the main fighter stations protecting London during World War II. Although the control tower was demolished, the fighter station is believed to be the best preserved of its kind, and the runway is still in its original configuration. It is still possible to walk around the airfield, and there is an annual air show.

GEORGE GILBERT SCOTT'S GODSTONE

DISTANCE/TIME	4.3 miles (6.9km) / 1hr 45min
ASCENT/GRADIENT	104ft (125m) / ▲ ▲
PATHS	Footpaths and bridleways can be muddy in places, 1 stile
LANDSCAPE	Sheltered, domestic landscape dotted with little ponds
SUGGESTED MAP	OS Explorer 146 Dorking, Box Hill & Reigate
START/FINISH	Grid reference: TQ350515
DOG FRIENDLINESS	Lead required on village roads, through churchyard, at Godstone Farm and requested at other points along route
PARKING	Adjacent to village pond, limited to 3 hours
PUBLIC TOILETS	Outside The Hare and Hounds pub, Godstone

Both churches on this route were restored by Sir George Gilbert Scott, one of the leading architects of the Victorian era – he headed the largest architectural practice of the time, and was associated with work on almost 500 churches. Students of the great man need hardly come to Godstone, when they can see many of his most famous buildings in London and other great cities. But, as you'll see, Godstone has one or two tricks up its sleeve. Sir George lived at Rook's Nest – now derelict and awaiting planning permission – less than a mile (1.6km) from the centre of the village (now on the site of a golf course).

Apart from his work on the local churches, he also designed one of Godstone's most charming buildings. You'll pass the mock-Tudor St Mary's Homes beside St Nicholas' Church. The almshouses were founded in 1872 by a young widow, Mrs Augusta Nona Hunt, for eight 'aged or infirm persons of good character'. With their profusion of little gabled windows, Sir George's designs seem almost to have grown out of the gardens between the Homes and Church Lane. A tiny chapel, with a fireplace in the west wall, completes the delightful group. Do look in and see it –it's open to visitors daily. The Homes became a housing association in 1982, and are now a registered charity.

Philistine or protector?

At about the time that he was building St Mary's Homes, Sir George was also involved in restoring St Nicholas' Church, and the Church of St Peter's in Tandridge. By now, some of his most famous projects – the Albert Memorial, the Home Office, and St Pancras Station in London – were already behind him. He had worked on many of the great cathedrals, too, but some people thought that his unusually thorough restorations destroyed too much of the original medieval work. A letter that Scott wrote from Rook's Nest in 1871 suggests a different story. In it, he told fellow architect George Edmund Street how he was under pressure from an Oxfordshire rector to tear out the old pews from his church: 'I value it no less for being humble,' he wrote. 'It is good old work and in its place, and I hold that it is wrong to renew it... I wish especially that it shall not be renewed against my will or after I am away.' So – was Sir George really the philistine he was often made out to be, or a conservationist at heart? Visit the churches on this route and judge for yourself.

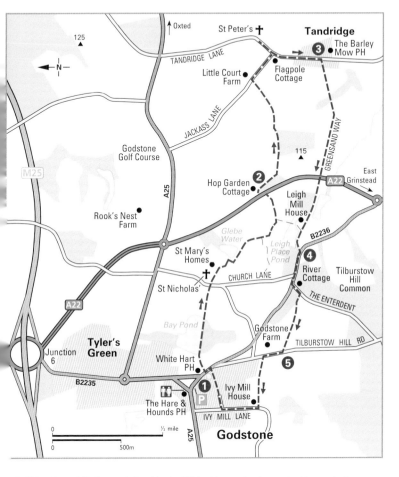

1. Take the public footpath beside the White Hart pub, signposted towards the church. Pass by Bay Pond and cross Church Lane and follow the path through the churchyard. Keep the church on your left, and continue along the winding path across two bridges as it passes Glebe Water. On reaching a field, turn right and soon turn through a gap in the hedge onto a gravel track. Turn left, passing a long low building, and then walk beside a large metal gate and continue ahead under the busy A22.

2. A few paces beyond the bridge, turn right at Hop Garden Cottage and follow the waymarked bridleway out onto Jackass Lane. Turn right here, opposite Little Court Farm, now converted into private houses. At the top of the hill, turn left for 100yds (91m) if you'd like to visit St Peter's Church. Otherwise

turn right, and follow Tandridge Lane to the public footpath on the right, just 30yds (27m) short of The Barley Mow pub.

3. Turn right and follow the broad, sandy track between open fields, and then a grassy track straight ahead to the kissing gate beside the A22. Cross the main road, and take the footpath, waymarked Greensand Way, directly opposite. A few paces further on, go through another kissing gate, signed GSW, to continue along the bridleway straight ahead, with a steep drop to a pond on your left. Jump the tiny ford (or use the footbridge) and walk up the lane past Leigh Place Pond as far as the B2236.

4. Leave the Greensand Way here and turn right. Follow the pavement until just beyond Church Lane, then turn left at the bus stop, up The Enterdent. After 100yds (91m), turn right onto the public footpath into the woods. The waymarked path climbs, steeply in places, to a kissing gate near the adventure playground on the edge of Godstone Farm. Follow the waymarked route through the farm grounds, to the stile on the north side of the car park, through a kissing gate, and follow as the path bends to meet the road.

5. Turn right onto Tilburstow Hill Road for 100yds (91m), then, just beyond the Godstone Farm delivery entrance, cross over and turn off left at the wooden footpath signpost. The path runs along the bottom of fields on the edge of Godstone village, then leads out into Ivy Mill Lane. Turn right for the short climb back to the village green, then right again into Ivy Mill Close, and follow the footpath back to the B road and the start of your walk.

Where to eat and drink

This walk is well-served by pubs. The Barley Mow in Tandridge is a large village pub serving Hall & Woodhouse beers, and offers a full range of food from bar snacks to à la carte. Dogs are welcome in the bar area and garden. In Godstone, the White Hart on the High Street has a light bites menu and main menu and serves a range of drinks from cocktails to ales. The Hare and Hounds on the Green also serves real ales, bar snacks and a full menu.

What to see

Close to the start of the walk, the Bay Pond is a peaceful haven for wildlife. But appearances can be deceptive, and these placid waters betray a warlike past. In Elizabethan times, gunpowder production was such an important local industry that one big mill nearby employed about a thousand workers. George Evelyn, father of the diarist John Evelyn, manufactured most of the gunpowder for the Crown's armed forces, and the pond was built in 1611 to provide water power.

While you're there

Godstone Farm is a popular children's farm with lots of friendly animals, sandpits, den building and adventure play areas. There's also an all-weather play barn. The farm is on Tilburstow Hill, just to the south of Godstone village, and also has a tea room. See www.godstonefarm.co.uk for more details.

OUTWOOD TO BLETCHINGLEY

DISTANCE/TIME	8.5 miles (13.6km) / 4hrs
ASCENT/GRADIENT	686ft (209m) / ▲ ▲
PATHS	Easy field edge paths and farm tracks, 9 stiles
LANDSCAPE	Rolling, sheep-grazed farmland dotted with small patches of woodland
SUGGESTED MAP	OS Explorer 146 Dorking, Box Hill & Reigate
START/FINISH	Grid reference: TQ326456
DOG FRIENDLINESS	Can run free but keep on lead near livestock
PARKING	National Trust car park opposite Outwood Mill
PUBLIC TOILETS	None on route

England was in the grip of the plague when Thomas Budgen of Nutfield built his mill on Outwood Common in 1665. And, according to tradition, the top of the newly completed mill was just the spot to watch the Great Fire sweeping through London the following year. Like any other mill, Outwood's sails will only turn when they are facing into the wind. So the 'post' mill is built around a huge vertical axle – or post – that allows the whole colossal structure to pivot. You'll see the oak post, reputedly brought from Crabbet Park, near Crawley, supported by a wooden framework resting on the four brick piers in the roundhouse. The body of the mill is almost 40ft (12m) high, and weighs around 25 tons, yet it's so well balanced that one person can turn it into the wind by pushing on the 'tailpole' at the back. The miller raises sacks to the top with a hoist, powered by the sails, and feeds the grain to the millstones on the floor below. The flour is then channelled to the spout floor at the bottom of the mill.

Outside, the great wooden sails are built from slats resembling a Venetian blind. This system was first patented many years after Outwood Mill was built, and must have replaced the original canvas sails. For all its grandeur, Thomas Budgen's masterpiece wasn't the only mill on this site. A new smock mill was built just yards away in 1790, following a family quarrel. With its four pairs of millstones and other modern equipment, it was designed to drive the old-fashioned post mill out of business. But the new miller was rather too fond of the nearby Bell Inn and, when ill fortune eventually led to the failure of his enterprise, the old post mill still soldiered on. The smock mill suffered the final indignity when it blew down during a storm in 1960.

As you head across the fields towards Bletchingley, with its castle and bustling High Street, even the sometimes intrusive presence of the nearby motorway can't disguise the medieval appearance of this landscape. Traditional sheep-grazed pasture gives way to a wooded route that curves around the foot of the castle earthworks and then climbs up to Bletchingley on the Greensand Way. The castle was built for the de Clares but destroyed some time after the Battle of Lewes in 1264. The moat still remains, and while it is on private land, the views of the moat along this route are accessible and free.

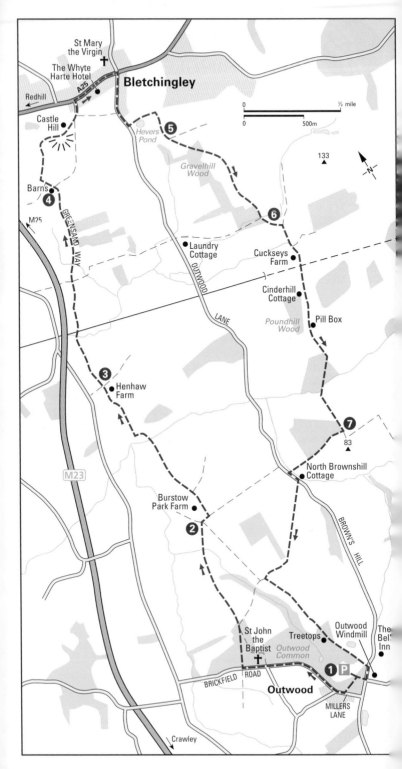

1. From the car park, follow the yellow waymark through the woods onto Millers Lane and then right into Brickfield Road. Turn right again down the woodland bridleway 180yds (165m) beyond the church, and follow it onto Outwood Common, through the trees and past a pond. Ignore a footpath on the right and continue ahead alongside the fields towards Burstow Park Farm.

2. Zig-zag right, then left, around the farmhouse to a gate. Walk along a wide grassy track in front of the farmhouse, through a second gate and then straight ahead through a kissing gate. Cross the field to another kissing gate and follow the field edge on your right to a stile next to a gate. Go through a kissing gate and across a concrete slab bridge. Bear half left to another kissing gate and plank bridge, go over a bridge and then bear left to a gap in the hedge, turn right up a field edge and cross three stiles to pass between the farm buildings.

3. Cross the farm drive, and continue over two stiles and through a couple of fields before crossing a stile and up steps to the railway line. Cross with care and descend to follow the fences on your left through three fields, to a metal gate alongside a wooden field gate. Go through a gate onto the Greensand Way and follow the route across the large pasture. Shortly after going through a gate and passing a couple of barns, the path divides.

4. Turn left and then right over a stile, up the slope on a fenced path and into a tunnel of low trees. Climb towards Castle Hill with fine views south, before emerging into Castle Square. Keep ahead to Bletchingley High Street and turn right and then right again, into Outwood Lane. After houses, turn left and left again, following a fingerpost around Hevers Pond onto a bridleway that winds uphill through a sunken way. Turn right at the brow, and follow the Greensand Way across an old concrete road, to a Telecoms manhole in 100yds (91m).

5. Branch right here, leaving the Greensand Way, along a footpath diagonally across a field into Gravelhill Wood. Beyond the wood, cross another field and go through a squeeze gate to follow the left-hand side of the next field. Just before the corner of this field, swing left through a gap in the hedge and walk diagonally across another field, heading towards the woods via a squeeze gate. Continue just inside the woodland edge, until you cross a small plank bridge.

6. At the bridleway, turn left and continue to Cukseys Farm and Cinderhill Cottage. Now follow the route just inside Poundhill Wood, passing a pill box on the left and, after another 0.75 miles (1.2km), emerge at the corner of a field.

7. Turn right here, along the woodland edge and onto the track leading out to Brown's Hill. Turn left, then shortly right through a kissing gate opposite North Brownshill Cottage, to head diagonally across three fields, with a stile between each. Bear gently right through a gap in the hedge, and continue through one field and into the next. After 40yds (37m), turn left through another gap and follow the left-hand field boundary into the woods on Outwood Common via a kissing gate. Join the drive at Treetops Cottage leading back to the start.

Where to eat and drink

The Bell Inn on Outwood Lane is a popular country pub. Children and dogs are welcome and there are real ales and home-cooked meals. The Bell also has a very pleasant garden.

CHALDON AND THE HAPPY VALLEY

DISTANCE/TIME	5.8 miles (9.3km) / 2hrs 45min
ASCENT/GRADIENT	515ft (157m) / ▲
PATHS	Well-maintained and signposted paths, 1 stile
LANDSCAPE	Downland and flower-rich grassland on Greater London's doorstep, some sections of woodland and working farmland
SUGGESTED MAP	OS Explorer 146 Dorking, Box Hill & Reigate
START/FINISH	Grid reference: TQ301571
DOG FRIENDLINESS	Some short sections where dogs must be on lead around livestock
PARKING	Car park on Farthing Downs, Ditches Lane, open dawn till dusk
PUBLIC TOILETS	Car park on Farthing Downs

Nearly everything about this walk is surprising. The map shows a small triangle of countryside, gripped between the fingers of London's suburban sprawl and cut short by the M25 motorway. Yet, as you leave the wide horizons of Farthing Downs and amble through the peaceful hay meadows of the Happy Valley and then along the North Downs Way towards Chaldon, you could be a hundred miles from the capital. If the countryside was lucky to escape development, your destination is even more remarkable. Inside Chaldon's church, the earliest known English wall painting was rediscovered on the west wall under a layer of whitewash, some seven centuries after it was created.

The walk begins in a stunning area of chalk downland, right on the Surrey border. Ironically, it was the Corporation of London that saved Farthing Downs from the expansion of London itself. Long before the Green Belt, the Corporation began protecting open spaces around the capital, and has owned and managed Farthing Downs since 1883. The Celts were growing crops on these downs by the time of Christ, but they quickly exhausted the thin soil and, by Saxon times, the area was being used for burials. When the winter sun shines low over the grass, you can make out some of the low banks marking Celtic field boundaries, as well as circular mounds covering the Saxon graves.

Heaven and hell

The graves in Chaldon churchyard are more recent, but the building itself dates from Saxon times and was mentioned in the Charter of Frithwald in the year 727. So the church was already old by the close of the 12th century when a travelling artist monk created its greatest treasure – the terracotta and cream mural of the Last Judgement on the west wall. Heaven and hell are divided by a horizontal layer of cloud. A ladder links the two scenes, and fortunate souls climb towards eternal bliss, while the damned tumble off into the flames below. You can read the full story of this grotesque and complex vision in a leaflet in the church, but the wonder is that the painting survived at all. Sometime around the 17th century the mural was whitewashed over, and it was only discovered during redecoration of the church in 1869, thanks to a sharp-eyed parish priest, who noticed colour on the wall, stopped the work and made sure the mural was protected. The scene was carefully cleaned and conserved in 1987, following a thorough overhaul of the church itself.

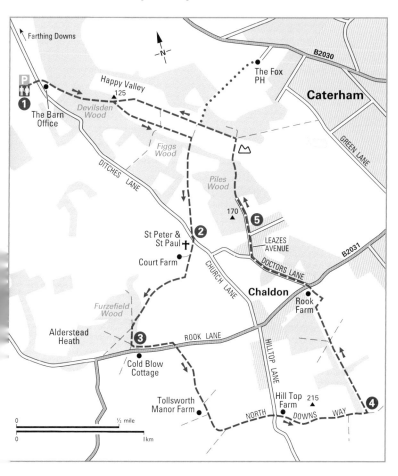

1. Cross Ditches Lane from the car park. Head down towards the trees, with stumps on your right, to pass The Barn Office and reach a public footpath signed 'Devilsden Wood/Happy Valley'. Turn right and follow the Downlands Circular Walk (DCW)/London Loop down through Devilsden Wood. At the fork, go left on the DCW. Beyond the woods, the Happy Valley opens up in front of you. Follow the woodland edge on your right until the path bears slightly left and begins to lose height. Now dodge right briefly into the woods, and follow the signposted path towards Chaldon Church (St Peter & St Paul). Soon you'll be back in the open, and you follow the woodland edge as far as a wooden footpath sign to the Church. Turn right here, and walk through the thin finger of Figgs Wood before crossing a large field.

2. At the far side of the field, turn left onto Ditches Lane; then, after 40yds (37m), fork right at the triangle to visit St Peter & St Paul church and see its remarkable mural. Return to Church Lane to pass the church, then, as the road swings right to Court Farm, cross the stile and take the path through the field towards Alderstead Heath. Cross two fields and leave via a gate into Furzefield Wood. Fork left 20yds (18m) beyond the gate onto a concrete path.

3. Just before you reach Rook Lane, turn left at a T-junction of concrete paths and ahead into the field, following the field edge path running parallel with the road as far as the kissing gate on the right. Cross the road and then follow the waymarked DCW onto the concrete drive towards Tollsworth Manor Farm. Continue ahead to pass the farmhouse. Stay with the blue signs of the Downlands Circular Walk as it dodges left and right off the concrete road, and follow it, with the hedge to your right. At the end of the field, the M23/M25 junction is visible below. Turn left here and join the North Downs Way National Trail. Cross Hilltop Lane and, after some 750yds (686m), reach a footpath signed towards Rook Lane, DCW.

4. Turn left off the North Downs Way and walk alongside fields on a fenced path and continue ahead to reach Rook Lane. Cross over and then keep straight on into Doctors Lane. Just past the pillar box, fork right into Leazes Avenue; then, 120yds (110m) further on, fork left at the little green, signposted towards the Happy Valley.

5. Continue to follow the waymarked route of the DCW as it drops down through Piles Wood to a footpath crossroads in the valley bottom. Turn left, towards Farthing Downs, and continue for 700yds (640m) along the grassy track. Should you feel thirsty, you can take the route to The Fox that crosses the valley at this point: turn right up a flight of steps and, at the top, follow the path to the right on a tarmac track, pass the car park and the pub is on your right. The round trip to the pub will add a mile (1.6km) to your walk. Otherwise, continue ahead then fork left at a grassy cross tracks and climb gently up the side of the valley to rejoin your outward route at the corner of Devilsden Wood. Retrace your footsteps to return to the car park.

Where to eat and drink

The Fox is a large London country pub, with stone-flagged floors and log fires in winter. It gets very busy but serves pretty good seasonal pub food. Families are welcome inside, but dogs only in the garden.

What to see

You'll hear the continuous, liquid song of the skylark long before you spot the speck that betrays its presence hundreds of feet above the grasslands of Farthing Downs. But it's worth scanning the skies for, because, after several minutes, you'll see it plummet to earth in a death-defying dive.

While you're there

Caterham's lively little East Surrey Museum regularly changes its displays: anything from local fossils and prehistoric flint tools to medieval pottery and Victoriana. There's also a room with special displays for children. The museum is open on Wednesday, Thursday and Saturday.

BANSTEAD AND THE CHIPSTEAD VALLEY

DISTANCE/TIME	3.4 miles (5.5km) / 1hr 30min
ASCENT/GRADIENT	453ft (138m) / ▲ ▲
PATHS	Woodland and field edge paths, muddy after rain, 4 stiles
LANDSCAPE	Wooded downland and working farmland
SUGGESTED MAP	OS Explorer 146 Dorking, Box Hill & Reigate
START/FINISH	Grid reference: TQ273583
DOG FRIENDLINESS	Can run free on Banstead Commons, although parts may be grazed; keep on lead around Perrotts Farm
PARKING	Holly Lane, Chipstead
PUBLIC TOILETS	None on route

The fight for London's countryside is nothing new, and the battle for Banstead Commons had the ingredients of a good Victorian melodrama – an evil Baronet, who was defeated in the nick of time by the fickle hand of fate.

Meet Sir John Hartopp MP, a Yorkshire baronet. In 1873, Sir John bought the Lordship of the Manor of Banstead, together with a huge area of land that included the Banstead Commons. You'll be walking through Park Downs, a part of his holding, to the north of Holly Lane. Most of the Commons were subject to grazing and other rights. This could have thwarted Sir John's plans for a housing development on Banstead Downs, and the sale of minerals from Banstead Heath. In practice, the rights were all but extinct, but Sir John began to consolidate his position by buying them up for himself. Determined to see some return on his investment, Hartopp raised his game. In 1876, he built a row of houses on Banstead Downs, and enclosed a part of Banstead Heath. The locals were furious, and formed the Banstead Commons Protection Society. They enlisted the help of the newly formed Commons Society, as well as the Corporation of London and the area's largest landowner, the Earl of Egmont.

In 1877, the protesters began court proceedings to challenge the enclosure of the heath, and a hugely expensive case dragged on until 1884. Just as a compromise seemed certain, fate intervened. Sir John's solicitors suddenly became insolvent, and Hartopp himself was dragged down with them. It strengthened the protesters' hand – but it delayed their ultimate victory until 1889. Realising that the future was far from secure, the commoners went on to petition for an Act of Parliament to protect the Commons. The result was the appointment of the Banstead Commons Conservators in 1893, and the Conservators continue to manage the area to this day.

But the countryside didn't always come out on top. When you cross over Holly Lane, you'll notice some mature houses on each side of the road. By coincidence, their story also begins in 1893, when Charles Garton bought the Banstead Wood Estate. He was destined to become Chairman of the

Parish Council, and the last of the area's big, patriarchal landowners. When Charles Garton died in 1934, the land on each side of Holly Lane was sold for development, and Banstead Wood House itself formed the basis of a new hospital. You can still see the hospital's tower from Park Downs, but in 2008 a new chapter in the estate's history began when it was sold and redeveloped into an elegant gated housing complex of more than a hundred homes.

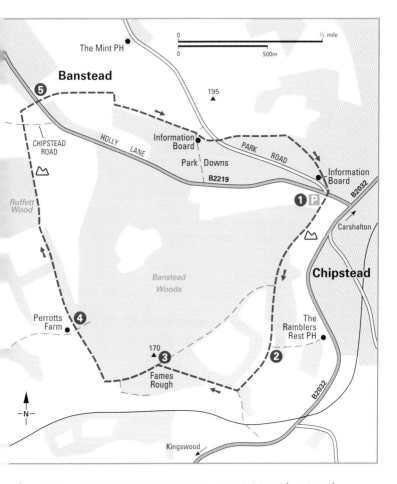

1. Leave the car park by the kissing gate at the top left-hand (southeast) corner and follow the waymarked gravel path. After 80yds (73m), join the public footpath signed towards Perrotts Farm. Just beyond, ignore the main track and fork left, waymarked Banstead Countryside Walk (BCW), just before the sculpture of a lion. The path climbs steadily through a tunnel of trees along the woodland edge. Look out for the old beeches on your right, nuzzling against one another and joined at the roots; these may once have formed part of an old boundary hedge.

2. Continue straight along the permissive path, between fields below and to your left, and an open area above and to your right. The path bears left to a

four-way junction; turn right to hug the fence running along pasture below to the left, signed 'Banstead Woods on BCW'. The path starts to climb deeper into the woods, passing some very large beech trees.

3. At a three-way fingerpost, turn left signed BCW. The path drops a little before rising again to reach a redundant stile in the corner of a field. Follow the field edge, keeping the woods on your right, to reach the buildings of Perrotts Farm.

4. Cross the stile here and the farm road, and take the footpath through a gate towards Holly Lane. Follow it between fields before arriving at Ruffett Wood. Walk the length of the wood, on your left-hand side, and past a redundant stile. At a three-way fingerpost, keep ahead signed to Holly Lane on the BCW. The path crosses the grandly named Chipstead Road – little more than a track. Pass the next redundant stile, before bearing right to soon meet Holly Lane.

5. Cross Holly Lane and continue along the public footpath, with hedgerow trees on your left and a field of crops on the right, sloping down to the road. At the corner of the field, turn right and then left into the trees at a fingerpost signed to Park Road, soon emerging onto the Downs on a grassy track, and head along the edge of Park Downs. Keep straight on at the information board, and cross over Park Road and follow the waymarked BCW. Turn right down the permissive footpath from the path, alongside fences on properties on the hillside, and reach the meeting point of Park Road and Holly Lane at an information board. Cross the roads back to the car park where you began.

Where to eat and drink

The Mint on Park Road in Banstead is a welcoming old pub, festooned with flower baskets in summer. The cosy stone-flagged bars have beamed ceilings and log fires, and there's real ale and a well-presented menu to suit all tastes; dogs are welcome. The Ramblers Rest in Chipstead will always be attractive to walkers. It is a large, sprawling half-timbered farmhouse complex with parts dating back to 1301.

What to see

Go quietly along the woodland edges and there's a good chance that you'll see an engaging little group of long-tailed tits. Listen for their thin *tseep-tseep* calls as they bounce restlessly through the trees in their distinctive black, white and pink plumage. These tiny birds roam the woods feeding on small insects, and they're the only common British birds of their size with such a long tail. Despite being only 5.5 inches (14cm) long – including a 3-inch (8cm) tail – they can travel as far as 25 miles (40.5km) in a day.

While you're there

Craggy Island Climbing and Caving Centre at Carshalton is one of the UK's largest indoor caving and bouldering centres, and welcomes experienced climbers and beginners with its huge range of graded climbs. Alternatively, you can crawl through a series of fantastic caves with plenty of fossils to look out for and tight squeezes to navigate. Visit www.craggy-island.com for opening and booking information.

WALTON HEATH AND BANSTEAD HEATH

DISTANCE/TIME	4.3 miles (6.9km) / 1hr 45min
ASCENT/GRADIENT	262ft (80m) / ▲
PATHS	Generally well-marked trails with some muddy tracks, and no steep hills
LANDSCAPE	Heathland and by the side of a golf course
SUGGESTED MAP	OS Explorer 146 Dorking, Box Hill & Reigate
START/FINISH	Grid reference: TQ246527
DOG FRIENDLINESS	Good, but keep under strict control by the golf course
PARKING	Margery Wood car park (charges for non-National Trust members)
PUBLIC TOILETS	None on route

The walk traverses Walton Heath and Banstead Heath, both of which have a long history – a medieval earthwork has been discovered on the northern part of Banstead Heath. For a long time, they have both been working heaths, and are now large open areas for walkers and other recreational users. The heathlands support a rich wildlife, including more than 200 different flowering plant species, and plenty of birds – including skylarks, Dartford warblers and woodlarks – as well as large numbers of butterflies.

Roman tiles

The history of Walton Heath goes back a long way, possibly to prehistoric times. There is evidence that it was occupied in Anglo-Saxon times, and Roman remains have been discovered on the heath, not far from the route of the walk. They have been excavated and covered up, so there is nothing to see now, unfortunately. However, Roman tiles can be seen on the walls of St Peter's Church in Walton. The church dates back to the 12th century, and has a lead font, which is said to be at least 800 years old. In Norman times, the manor was given to a prominent nobleman, and was later acquired by Henry VIII, who then gave it to Catherine of Aragon. There is a rumour that Anne of Cleves stayed in the manor house, and that Henry VIII may have visited her there.

One of the houses in the area was built for Lloyd George (Prime Minister from 1916 to 1922), who enjoyed playing golf on Walton Heath Golf Course, as did several other prominent parliamentarians, including Arthur Balfour and Andrew Bonar Law. Winston Churchill was also a member, and the club's first captain was Edward, Prince of Wales, who became King Edward VIII (briefly). In 1913, Lloyd George had a weekend house built in Walton. Before the house was finished, however, a bomb placed by suffragettes went off, severely damaging the servants' quarters. Emily Pankhurst accepted responsibility. Lloyd George survived and his house was eventually finished. He was so keen on playing golf at Walton that some felt World War I was run from there.

A few miles west of Walton is the village of Headley, where there are also houses with interesting connections. Perhaps best known is Headley Court, the medical centre for members of the armed forces, from where so many stories of heroic rehabilitation emanate. More prosaically, Headley Grove has been owned over the years by Sir Malcolm Campbell and Terry-Thomas, the actor.

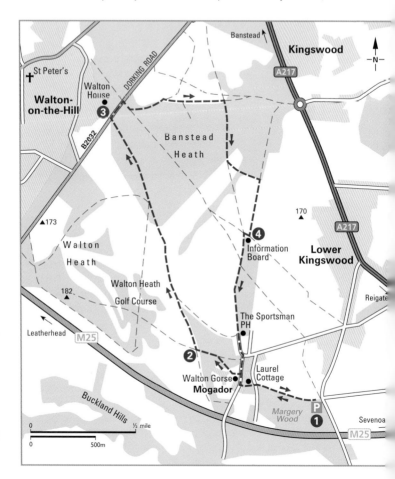

1. From the car park entrance, turn left and left again to take the path parallel to the side of the car park, with an open field and farm to the right, following the bridleway sign. Reach a small road, Margery Grove, and go straight on along the public bridleway beside Laurel Cottage. At the next road crossing, turn right along a public bridleway. Pass Walton Gorse on the left and take the next public bridleway to the left. Cross a driveway and continue straight on, following the public bridleway sign. At a T-junction of tracks, turn left, signed to Chequers Lane.

2. At the subsequent cross-tracks, just before the golf course and signed Walton-on-the Hill, turn right past a white-painted coal post and walk alongside Walton Heath Golf Course. At a field, the public bridleway goes left,

and you continue along it between trees. Ignore the permissive horse ride to the right and continue straight ahead with woodland on the right and the golf course to the left. The path then meets the B2032 Dorking Road.

3. Cross the road with care and turn right along the pavement. On reaching the public bridleway sign, cross over the road again and follow the bridleway straight ahead. Where the path forks, bear left and continue, ignoring paths to left and right. Emerge from a copse into an open field and take the bridleway to the right, around the right-hand edge of a wood. Ignore the paths on the right and, on meeting a cross-track, turn right and follow the permissive ride track. Where the path forks, take the left fork, still following the permissive ride sign on the fingerpost, and, at the next cross-track, go straight ahead. Emerge from the woodland onto a common with a barrier to your left and go straight on, crossing a permissive ride. Continue along the path down to the left into woodland, following the sign for the permissive ride. After walking through a copse, enter an open field and continue straight ahead to the top of it. Bear right along a grassy path to meet a track running along the field edge, near a bench, and continue along the boundary to a notice board.

4. Facing the front of the notice board, go ahead and then, after 30yds (27m), turn left through the gap and then left along the edge of a wood, with a field to the right. Meet a road and pass The Sportsman pub on the left. Follow the road round to the right and, on passing Walton Gorse, turn left and retrace your outward walk back to the car park.

Where to eat and drink

The Sportsman pub is on the return section of this walk. It has been an inn since the 16th century, when it would have been visited by royalty when out hunting. Today it is a smart, stylish pub and restaurant, providing good-quality food with friendly service. There is plenty of space in the garden to enjoy when the weather permits.

What to see

At intervals along this walk there are white metal posts bearing the coat of arms of the City of London. These are coal posts and marked the territory of about 15 miles (24km) around London, beyond which taxes were charged on coal and wine that were brought into the city. They were set up around 1861, and over 200 still survive.

While you're there

Reigate Fort, originally built in 1898 as protection against a possible invasion by the French, has been excellently restored by the National Trust. Its purpose was to store tools and ammunition, and it is possible to explore the magazine, the casement and the fort itself.

REIGATE HEATH
AND THE MOLE VALLEY

DISTANCE/TIME	4.3 miles (7km) / 2hrs 15min
ASCENT/GRADIENT	397ft (121m) / ▲
PATHS	Rural paths, bridleways and village roads, 3 stiles
LANDSCAPE	Lowland landscape in Mole Valley
SUGGESTED MAP	OS Explorer 146 Dorking, Box Hill & Reigate
START/FINISH	Grid reference: TQ238501
DOG FRIENDLINESS	Take care at the village road crossings, and keep on lead across farmland and golf course
PARKING	Car park at Reigate Heath, Flanchard Road
PUBLIC TOILETS	None on route

Reigate Heath is one of the last remaining areas of natural heathland in Surrey, and is both a local nature reserve and a Site of Special Scientific Interest. Most notably, these heather and acid grass heathlands are home to the rare Serotine bat, as well as a colony of southern marsh orchids. They are also the backdrop to a rich and rather intriguing history, and walking across Reigate Heath with its wide views and rolling landscapes, you soon realise that this is a special place. Here you'll find Bronze Age burial mounds, fine houses such as Wonham Manor, and wartime pill boxes scattered across the landscape. It is a place where tales of highwaymen and hangmen abound.

Galley Hill windmill

Standing on Galley Hill (home to a gibbet until 1817), you'll also find what is believed to be the only windmill in the world that is also a consecrated chapel. The windmill dates from around 1765, and was once one of six mills in the area – only two remain, and you'll find the other, Wray Common Windmill, on nearby Batts Hill.

The mill was operational for more than 100 years, and when it fell into disuse was converted into a chapel of ease for St Mary's Parish Church, Reigate. The first service took place on 14 September 1880. In 1900, its new owner, Reigate Golf Course (which also did much work to preserve and repair the mill), leased the mill to the church. New sails were fitted in 1927, but when they blew off again in 1943, they proved too expensive to replace. Despite ongoing repairs and maintenance, a survey revealed that although the roundhouse was in a good condition, the mill was not and, in 1962, it was purchased by Reigate Borough Council. Over the next two years the mill was renovated and new sails fitted, with further restoration in 2002. Today the sails no longer turn, and it isn't open to the public. But you can visit the church and take a look at the massive crosstrees and quarterbars that support the structure above. Occasional services are still held in the church.

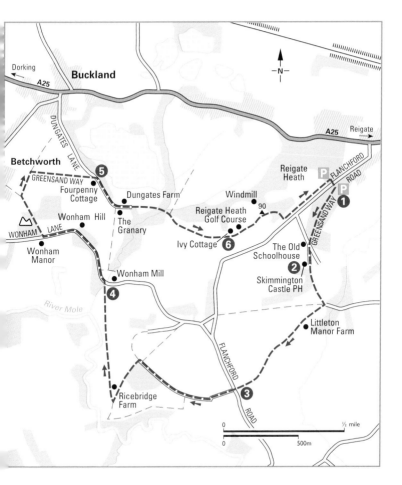

1. Take the path from the top corner of the car park on the eastern side of Flanchford Road, by a large oak tree, and turn right on a sandy path that soon broadens. Follow it into the trees and then continue across the golf course, heading towards houses, to reach a road. Turn left opposite The Old Schoolhouse, towards the Skimmington Castle pub. Before you reach the pub, turn left onto the public bridleway, which then skirts around the pub and car park.

2. Head through the trees with paddocks on your right. At the lane, turn right onto the driveway, and go through a gate towards Littleton Manor Farm. After the barn, bear right and continue ahead to pass farmhouses on your left, then continuing onto a fenced path between paddocks. Before the track bends right, cross the stile straight ahead and then turn left on a path beside a fence and young staked trees and bushes. Cross a stile to Flanchford Road.

3. Cross straight over and keep ahead on the signed public byway opposite. Continue on this broad gravel track to pass a house and barn on your left, a hand-painted sign points ahead to Ricebridge Farm. Continue on the same track, and, at a four-way signpost, turn left, with the woods on your left and

a field right. Just past Ricebridge Farm, turn right over a waymarked stile to follow the public footpath along the right-hand field edge. Continue on the waymarked path as it leads between a wartime pill box and the hedge, crossing a stream before heading through an open field, with more pill boxes, to a kissing gate. Pass through and then cross the bridge to emerge on Wonham Lane, opposite Wonham Mill (now converted into housing).

4. Turn left and keep going straight ahead, uphill to pass houses on your right, then railings on your left. Before the gated entrance to Wonham Manor, turn right through a gate on a signed bridleway and head steeply uphill into woodland. Emerge to continue between a post-and-wire fence, with a field on your left. At a four-way footpath sign, turn right through a kissing gate onto the Greensand Way and follow the field edge through a second kissing gate. Continue to a third kissing gate and emerge onto Dungates Lane by Fourpenny Cottage.

5. Turn right and continue, passing The Granary cottage on your right and Dungates Farm on your left. Just after you cross a stream, turn right, signed The Greensand Way, and continue to the edge of Reigate Heath Golf Course, beside Ivy Cottage.

6. Cross the golf course with care (heading towards the windmill), then climb the low, heather-clad hill towards the clubhouse and windmill. Turn left through the car park and then, with Golf Cottage on your left, turn right down a path, and then right again on a sandy track. Just before reaching the road, turn left and follow the path parallel to the road all the way back to the car park.

Where to eat and drink

At Reigate Heath, the Skimmington Castle pub keeps dog biscuits behind the bar. Nowadays, you'll find real ales and a good range of bar food, from snacks to main meals, served in the traditional cosy interior with its huge fireplace. Children and dogs will find a warm welcome, and there is good outside space.

What to see

Dating from 1485, the chimney of the Skimmington Castle pub was used as a lookout by highwaymen on the heath. A gibbet stood nearby on Galley Hill, and local legend tells how one of the former landlords of the Black Horse pub in West Street, Dorking, was hanged there after being convicted of highway robbery.

While you're there

St Michael's churchyard on Wonham Lane played a starring role as St John's Church, Stoke Clandon, in the film *Four Weddings and a Funeral*. Pop around to the lychgate on the north side of the church, and you'll probably recall seeing Charles and Scarlett (Hugh Grant and Charlotte Coleman) frantically changing their clothes after a last-minute dash to Angus and Laura's wedding.

A CIRCUIT FROM CHARLWOOD

DISTANCE/TIME	4.3 miles (6.9km) / 1hr 45min
ASCENT/GRADIENT	262ft (80m) / ▲▲
PATHS	Byways and woodland paths, short sections on village roads and farmland, 8 stiles
LANDSCAPE	Well-wooded, agricultural scenery
SUGGESTED MAP	OS Explorer 146 Dorking, Box Hill & Reigate
START/FINISH	Grid reference: TQ243410
DOG FRIENDLINESS	Keep on lead along roads and through Greenings Farm
PARKING	On The Street in Charlwood, opposite the recreation ground
PUBLIC TOILETS	None on route

Even non-plane spotters will confess to a certain frisson of excitement every time they see a big jet dropping smoothly onto the tarmac, or climbing steeply off the runway like a rocket. It's an awesome business – and that's before you consider the logistics of handling the passengers. Gatwick Airport may now be in Sussex (it was part of Surrey until 1974), but there's no escaping its day-to-day impact on this corner of Surrey. So, rather than ignore the area completely, let's take a decent look at the place. You'll see plenty of aircraft on this walk, which passes within 0.5 miles (800m) of the end of the runway.

Gatwick Manor

The airport itself may be a child of the 20th century, but the name Gatwick goes back to 1241, when Richard de Warwick assigned the rights over 22 acres (8.9ha) of land in the Manor of Cherlewood (Charlwood) to one John de Gatwyck. The land subsequently became part of the Manor of Gatwick, and remained in the same family until the 14th century. In 1495, the Manor of Gatwick was sold to the Jordan family and William Jordan built a fine and spacious new house at Gatwick, which replaced the old manor house, just to the east of Povey Cross (near the current airport). It was built in the style of William and Mary. The house was still standing until 1950, when it was demolished, and the site of the manor now lies under the buildings of Gatwick's North Terminal. The nearby Gatwick Manor Hotel was never the Gatwick Manor. It was, in fact, another historic house of interest called Hyderhurst, which was the home of one Richard de Hyde.

Taking flight

The Surrey Aero Club purchased a piece of Gatwick land in 1930, and the Air Ministry issued the airport's first commercial licence in 1934. Scheduled services began from Gatwick Airport in May 1936 – at that time a single fare to Paris cost four pounds and five shillings, and the price included the rail fare from London. The airport was requisitioned during World War II, and post-war operations resumed when Queen Elizabeth II opened London's new £7.8m airport in June 1958. Today, Gatwick operates as the busiest single-runway airport in the world. Over 90 airlines carry more than 32 million passengers a year to some 200 destinations worldwide. On average, an aircraft lands or takes off every two minutes of each day, all year round, and the airport generates employment for around 23,000 people.

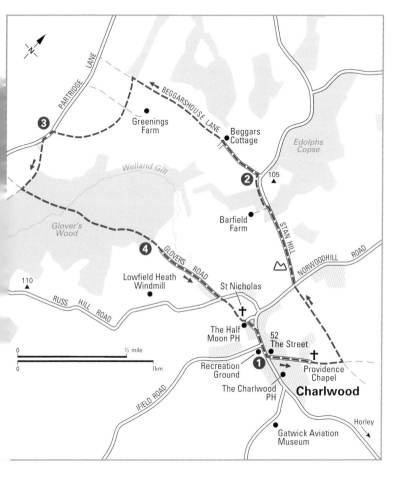

1. With the recreation ground on your right, walk past 52 The Street and turn left up Chapel Road. Continue onto the byway and pass the extraordinary Providence Chapel (currently undergoing restoration). Behind the low picket fence, a few tombstones lean drunkenly to the side of this small, weather-boarded chapel with its wooden veranda. The building, which dates from 1816, is straight out of an advert for Jack Daniels, and seems to have dropped in from Kentucky. Go through a gate and turn left at the byway crossroads towards Stan Hill. When the gravel track bends right, continue ahead through a metal gate and straight across Norwoodhill Road. At the brow of the hill, take the signposted footpath on the left, just beyond the entrance to Barfield Farm.

2. The path leads to the corner of Beggarshouse Lane, where you turn left and follow the lane onto the tree-lined byway. At the woods beyond the buildings of Greenings Farm, turn left just after entering the woods over a plank bridge and waymarked stile. Follow the left-hand edge of an open field, then cross the farm lane at a pair of waymarked stiles and plank bridges. Continue over another pair of stiles and plank bridges until the hedge bears left at a stile. Don't go over it, but steer right here towards the stile in the far corner of the field, then head across the next field to the stile into Partridge Lane.

3. Turn left for 75yds (69m) before turning left again onto the signposted bridleway. Soon the path dodges into Glover's Wood and, 200yds (183m) further on, a few paces before a waymarker post marking a woodland crossroads, turn hard left on a footpath, then continue to follow the waymarked footpath across Welland Gill via steps and a bridge, and carry on to the far side of the woods.

4. Leave the woods via a kissing gate, then continue ahead on a short, fenced path between fields and through a second gate down onto Glovers Road. Cross Rectory Lane/Russ Hill Road and keep straight on down the footpath opposite. The path passes St Nicholas Church – but you should take time to look inside this welcoming church, as there are some of the finest medieval wall paintings in the country. Most poignant is a hunting scene, fairly common in artwork from around the time of the Black Death, in which three youths encounter three skeletons. 'As you are, we were,' say the skeletons, before adding, 'as we are, you will be...' Beyond the churchyard, turn right past The Half Moon pub, then right again for the last 100yds (91m) back to the recreation ground.

Where to eat and drink

Try 52 The Street for coffee and cake, an all-day breakfast or a hot meal. Also on The Street in Charlwood is The Half Moon, an intimate, low-beamed village local tracing its origins back to the 15th century. They serve real ales, and dogs are welcome. Further down the same road, The Charlwood is a gastro pub serving food from 9am to 9pm, six days a week.

What to see

Look out for the sails of Lowfield Heath Windmill. It was built about 1740, and ground flour until about 1880. When its site at Lowfield Heath was needed for expansion at Gatwick Airport it was dismantled and moved to its present site in 1988. Ten years later, in 1998, the mill ran for the first time in nearly 120 years. The windmill is run by volunteers; check www.lowfieldheathwindmill.co.uk for opening hours.

While you're there

Gatwick Aviation Museum, just outside the village to the southeast, has a collection of vintage classic aircraft. The museum is open Friday to Sunday all year round; visit www.gatwick-aviation-museum.co.uk for more information.

LEIGH AND THE UPPER MOLE VALLEY

DISTANCE/TIME	4.2 miles (6.8km) / 2hrs
ASCENT/GRADIENT	141ft (43m) / ▲
PATHS	Field edge and cross-field paths, 14 stiles
LANDSCAPE	Low-lying, small-scale agricultural scenery
SUGGESTED MAP	OS Explorer 146 Dorking, Box Hill & Reigate
START/FINISH	Grid reference: TQ224469
DOG FRIENDLINESS	Keep on lead near livestock; extra care required where bulls may be grazing in fields along the route
PARKING	Layby between The Plough and church in Leigh
PUBLIC TOILETS	None on route

Leigh is one of those places that seems happy for history to pass it by. Indeed, part of its charm is that so little seems to have happened here recently. The walk starts on the picturesque village green, where the pub, church and adjoining Priest's House all have their origins in the 15th century. Just up the road, Leigh Place may be older still; but in 1530 it was sold to Edward Shelley, an ancestor of the Romantic poet. The sale deed records the village as 'Lye' – and that's how the name is pronounced. In Tudor times, Leigh was in the heart of Surrey's Black Country. There was a small iron-smelting furnace or 'bloomery', with water-powered hammers, near Hammer Bridge, to the south of Clayhill Farm. Later the dramatist Ben Jonson is said to have lived at Swain's Farm; but by then the place was so quiet that an early 20th-century writer wondered what on earth he could have found to do there.

What's the point?

To put Leigh on the map, you must climb to the top of the low hill above Swains Farm. Here, about a mile into your walk, you'll come to a curious concrete pillar standing aloof near the middle of the field. The column is just one of around 6,500 'triangulation pillars' that, until very recently, formed the basic framework for all Ordnance Survey mapping. Triangulation relies on a network of triangles with precisely measured sides and angles, like the frame of those glass geodesic domes that were popular in the 1970s.

It all started in the reign of George III, when Major General William Roy was commissioned by the Royal Society to measure the first baseline on Hounslow Heath, now the site of Heathrow Airport. Roy had campaigned for a national mapping authority, but he died in 1790, a year before the Ordnance Survey was founded. The new organisation built on Roy's work to complete the triangulation of Great Britain, and published its first one-inch-to-the-mile maps during the early years of the 19th century. These were to become the Ordnance Survey's flagship products, until they were replaced by the modern

Landranger maps in the mid-1970s. On the top of the triangulation pillar, you'll see the metal fitment where generations of surveyors have fixed their theodolites to check the location of similar pillars on the surrounding hills. But time marches on and satellite-based global positioning systems (GPS) have transformed map-making technology, consigning most of these hilltop pillars to the history books. Leigh can once more return to its slumbers.

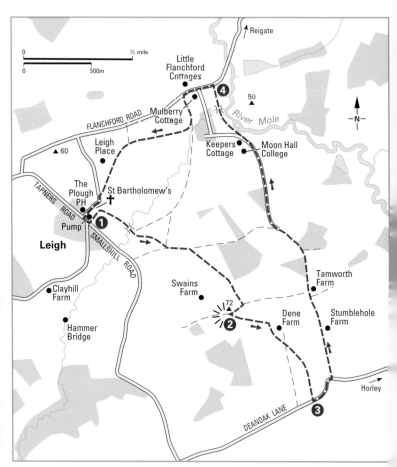

1. Start at the village pump on the green and take the signed footpath through the churchyard, through a kissing gate and then across a field to reach a footbridge. Cross the brook, and the waymarked stile and plank bridge 40yds (37m) further on, then continue with the hedge on your right to just beyond the far corner of the field. Cross the stile and plank bridge and turn left onto the blue-waymarked bridleway. After 100yds (91m), continue ahead, bearing right through a waymarked gate, and immediately turn half right across the field to a stile. Cross the next field to a stile besided a wood at the base of a small slope. Turn right over a stile, and up a short hill beside the woods. At the brow, you'll come to a stile; don't cross it, but turn right, towards the triangulation pillar (or trig point) across the field. There are some fine views from here.

2. Turn hard left at the triangulation pillar and double back to the far corner of the field. If you keep straight on beside the hedge you were following earlier, you are trespassing! Cross the stile in the corner of the field, then follow the succession of three waymarked stiles, two of which are alongside the driveway to Dene Farm, then cross the farm drive. Bear half right here, and cross the field to a plank bridge and stile. Continue through the next field and out onto Deanoak Lane.

3. Turn left. Then, just beyond the double bend, turn left again, up the lane towards Stumblehole Farm. Follow the lane straight past Stumblehole and Tamworth farms and through a small patch of woodland, then bear left at the three-way signpost onto a concrete/gravel road. Continue past Moon Hall College; then, 55yds (50m) beyond Keepe's Cottage, look out for a waymarked stile on your right. Cross this and bear away beside the infant River Mole. Once through the gap, turn sharp right and over a wooden footbridge, with a stile at either end, across a field and stile then out onto Flanchford Road.

4. Turn left to reach Little Flanchford Cottages. A few paces further on, take the footpath on your left, and cross a footbridge and then a stile after 150yds (137m). Bear right over a footbridge and follow the hedge on the right-hand side, over a stile and beneath the power lines and into a third field. Walk diagonally to your left across the fourth field, to a kissing gate. Turn left here for the last 100yds (91m) along the road and back to the start.

Where to eat and drink

The Plough in Leigh is your stereotypical English country pub, with its pretty flower tubs and pleasant garden. White weatherboarded and tile-hung, it sits overlooking the village green. There's a wide range of traditional ales behind the bar and lots of eating options, from bar snacks to restaurant meals. It's open all day every day. Dogs are welcome in the public bar and garden, and children in the restaurant and garden.

What to see

The west end of St Bartholomew's Church has a remarkable history. Much of the church dates from around 1430, when the building was given a low stone tower and weatherboarded belfry. It stood for more than four centuries, until it was replaced by a larger tower when the church was restored in 1855. But the new tower didn't last. In 1890, it was swept away in a dramatic remodelling, which extended the nave and added the western porch and shingled spire that you see today.

While you're there

To the southeast at Handcross, just over the border in Sussex, is the romantic Nymans, a 20th-century garden set around an atmospheric house and ruins. The estate was purchased by Ludwig Messel in the late 1800s, and he created his dream home and gardens here. The house was partly destroyed in a fire in 1947, but the Gothic mansion remains and the estate is now in the care of the National Trust. There is a plant centre and café as well as guided walks and talks in the garden and woods, a small gallery with changing exhibitions, and a secondhand bookshop.

EPSOM DOWNS AND THE RACECOURSE

DISTANCE/TIME	5.2 miles (8.4km) / 2hrs
ASCENT/GRADIENT	492ft (150m) / ▲
PATHS	Mainly broad, easy-to-follow bridleways
LANDSCAPE	Open skies of Downs and wooded landscape
SUGGESTED MAP	OS Explorer 146 Dorking, Box Hill & Reigate
START/FINISH	Grid reference. TQ224584
DOG FRIENDLINESS	Lead required before midday, when racehorses train on the Downs
PARKING	Car park by mini-roundabout on Tattenham Corner Road (charges apply on race days)
PUBLIC TOILETS	200yds (183m) west of car park, towards grandstand

There's always a holiday atmosphere on Epsom Downs. With the ice cream vans, the wind in your face and the huge, wide skies, the Downs have everything but sea and sand. There's a long tradition of recreation on Epsom Downs. In 1660, Samuel Pepys' diary records daily horseraces at midday, with wrestling, cudgel playing, hawking and foot racing in the afternoons. Hare coursing was also popular, based on an enclosed warren established by Lord Baltimore in 1720. You'll see two of the old gateposts to the Warren on your right, as you walk down beside the gallops a mile or so into your walk.

And they're off!

You'll start by crossing the racecourse itself. The first formal race meeting took place in 1661 in the presence of King Charles II, but it was a young man of 21 who was destined to establish the most famous names in Epsom's sporting calendar. In 1773, the 12th Earl of Derby bought The Oaks, a country house at nearby Woodmansterne. He and his friends were keen followers of racing, and, in 1779, they inaugurated 'The Oaks' – a new race for three-year-old fillies. Spurred on by the success of the new race, the Earl and his friend Sir Charles Bunbury promoted another short distance event the following year. The Earl won the toss for the honour of naming the contest, though Sir Charles consoled himself when his horse, Diomed, actually won the race. The Epsom Derby had been born.

But what of the spectators? To begin with there were minimal facilities, and the 18th-century crowds simply gathered on the hill. Enter the property speculator Charles Bluck, described as a 'rogue and a rascal, an unscrupulous knave, the biggest villain to go unhanged'. Bluck charmed the Lord of the Manor with his plans for a new £5,000 grandstand, and quickly obtained the lease to a prime 1-acre (0.4ha) site. This upstaged the newly formed Epsom Grandstand Association, and there was a good deal of wheeling and dealing before the Association completed its stand in 1830. Building lasted for almost a century, until the site was redeveloped in 1927. The new Queen's Stand, added in 1992, includes facilities for conferences, dances and corporate hospitality, and in 2009 the Duchess of Cornwall opened the Duchess Stand. The focus is firmly on horseracing at Epsom, but there's a range of events all year round; visit www.epsom.thejockeyclub.co.uk for dates and times.

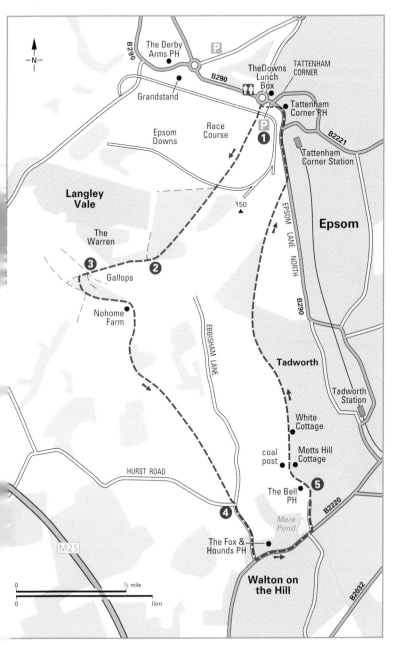

1. From the roundabout near The Downs Lunch Box, take the signposted bridleway to Walton Road. Cross the racecourse and continue along the broad, waymarked lane, keeping an eye out for any cars. The bridleway remains open on race days, though naturally there are some restrictions during the races.

2. Walk alongside and then within a wood. When the lane swings hard right, follow the bridleway that forks off down a narrow path to the left. Bear right at the gallops, before rejoining the broader lane, at a fingerpost, down past The Warren. There's a lovely view across the valley from here.

3. At the bottom of the hill, on the edge of the woodland, lies a six-way junction. Think of it as a mini-roundabout, and take the third exit, straight ahead. It's a narrow track through scrubby trees, but it soon leads you out onto a broader bridleway. Turn left and then, in a few paces, ignore the track on the right, signed to Walton Road, and keep straight on at the bridleway signpost, towards Walton on the Hill, and follow the waymarked track as it swings right at Nohome Farm and begins the climb out of the valley on a narrow path.

4. The bridleway ends at the junction of Hurst Road and Ebbisham Lane. Keep ahead on Ebbisham Lane and turn left at the bottom into Walton Street. Pass The Fox and Hounds pub and Mere Pond, then turn left at The Bell pub sign, up the side of the pond. After 30yds (27m), fork right at Withybed Corner and follow the lane to The Bell.

5. Keep straight ahead, signed to Motts Hill Lane, to pass a white metal coal post and barrier. Turn right down a path alongside Motts Hill Cottage, to rejoin the lane at White Cottage (right-hand side). As the lane bears right, turn left onto the bridleway along the backs of gardens. At the junction of paths, bear left and then right up the slope at the information board. At the top of the slope, follow a fingerpost heading towards Epsom Lane North. Cross the road, and continue along the grassy verge, bearing right to cross Tattenham Crescent, and return to the car park.

Where to eat and drink

Just across the road from the car park you'll see The Downs Lunch Box kiosk and the large Tattenham Corner pub/restaurant overlooking the course. Tucked away behind the grandstand, The Derby Arms is quieter and more intimate, though still with the emphasis on food. At the other end of your walk, The Fox and Hounds in Walton on the Hill is your best bet for a bite of lunch. You'll also pass The Bell, a small, intimate pub tucked away from the road at Withybed Corner.

What to see

Epsom's chalk downlands support some rare plants, including the round-headed rampion with its purple blooms, bastard toadflax with its distinctive star-shaped flowers, and the delicate chalkhill eyebright.

While you're there

Children will love a visit to Hobbledown in Epsom. It has a wide range of animals, including meerkats, maras, otters, ponies, donkeys and alpacas. There's a range of climbing and indoor play areas, as well as Hobbledown Village and Market to explore, with refreshments available at 'Hobnosh'.

EXPLORING HEADLEY HEATH

DISTANCE/TIME	4.6 miles (7.4km) / 2hrs 30min
ASCENT/GRADIENT	712ft (217m) / ▲▲
PATHS	Mainly woodland tracks
LANDSCAPE	Wooded heathland and chalk valleys
SUGGESTED MAP	AA Walker's Map 23 Guildford, Farnham & The Downs
START/FINISH	Grid reference: TQ205538
DOG FRIENDLINESS	Under strict control near grazing animals on heath
PARKING	National Trust car park, Headley Heath on B2033, Headley Common Road (free to NT members)
PUBLIC TOILETS	None on route

Look around you, for this is no ordinary place. About a tenth of all the world's lowland heaths are found in southern England, and Headley includes the largest remaining area of acid heathland on the North Downs. Although heathland is an artificial habitat, it's home to many rare and threatened species. Go quietly and you may see stonechats, woodlarks and even the occasional Dartford warbler. Common lizards live here too, as well as slow worms – harmless silvery legless lizards, not snakes, as is often thought.

The name Headley means 'a heather clearing surrounded by woodland', and that's pretty much what you'll see here today. But around 8,000 years ago, this was a very different landscape. At that time most of Britain was covered with dense woodland, and without human intervention that's how it would have stayed. Things altered when Neolithic people arrived in about 6000 BC, slashing and burning the forest to provide grazing for their animals. At Headley, they found just what they wanted: high ground, with an easily worked sandy soil. It was the beginning of organised farming, and in one way or another the land has been grazed here ever since. Well, almost.

During World War II, Headley Heath was used as a training area by the Canadian Army. Their tanks and earth-moving equipment destroyed the open vegetation, and, after the war, birch trees started to invade the disturbed ground. Now Headley Heath is the setting for a very different type of warfare – the constant battle against encroaching woodland. You'll see the National Trust's secret weapon as you explore. The black and white belted Galloway cattle are very friendly and roam freely over the heathland so don't be surprised if you meet them on this walk. Ten of these natural lawnmowers keep down the scrub and help maintain the special habitats of the heath. To discover their favourite grazing areas and explore the many habitats of the heath, including the 'Bug Hotel' at Aspen Pond and the chalk-loving plants near The Pyramids, try the National Trust's short Lizard Trail. This is marked with orange markers from the car park, where you'll also find a map and directions.

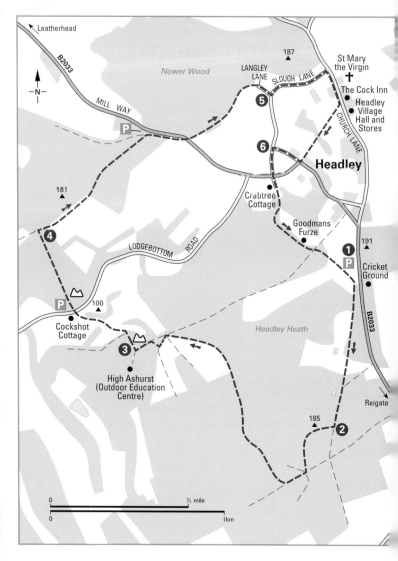

1. Face the road, walk to the far right-hand corner of the car park, and take the bridleway on your right passing through a gate, following the blue-topped posts and past two ponds on the right. Ignore all paths left and right until reaching a junction of paths with blue- and purple-topped posts.

2. Turn right here, and follow the bridleway for 125yds (115m) to a junction. Take the first left and at the next junction of bridleways turn right, rising slightly. At cross-tracks, walk straight ahead, still following the blu- topped posts. The broad track starts to descend to the valley bottom with a clear valley side to your right. Reach a junction of paths, with steps ahead of you, turn left here and pass another flight of steps on your left. Continue ahead, still on a bridleway, and after 100yds (91m) turn right, climbing steeply up an eroded path alongside a post-and-wire fence. At the top, pass through a gate

and immediately take the path on the right. If you reach the road at High Ashurst, you'll know that you've gone too far.

3. Double back to the right, and wind your way down out of the woods. Cross Lodgebottom Road at Cockshot Cottage, jink left and climb the narrow bridleway, occasionally very steeply, to a T-junction with a level track.

4. Turn right, and follow the public bridleway as far as Mill Way, alongside a paling fence with fine views to your right over the wooded valley. Just short of the road, bear right onto the public bridleway and follow it until it leads you across the road and onto a signposted byway. Follow the byway and continue on Langley Lane to the junction.

5. Fork left here, into Slough Lane, and walk up to the junction with Church Lane. Turn right onto the permissive bridleway that runs beside the road. Opposite The Cock Inn, turn right at the bus stop onto a signposted footpath. Follow it through to a road junction, turn hard right into Tot Hill Lane, and drop down to the junction with a metalled road.

6. Turn left and cross Mill Way into Crabtree Lane. Follow the waymarked bridleway past Crabtree Cottage and up the hill, through a gate, to a pit on your left-hand side. Bear left here, along the blue-waymarked track. Pass Goodmans Furze on your left and continue ahead, until you see the car park between trees on your left-hand side. Turn left through a gate to the car park.

Where to eat and drink

Three-quarters of the way round the walk you'll come to The Cock Inn, next to Headley Church. This has a spacious bar and terrace and serves a good range of food. Next door is Headley Village Hall and Stores, with a tea room, drinks and hot snacks to take away. Occasionally there will be a refreshments van in the car park or an ice cream van in summer.

What to see

Headley churchyard boasts an odd little grotto – the Faithfull family vault. Ferdinand Faithfull was Rector of Headley during the mid-19th century; Emily Faithfull, who was born at Headley's Old Rectory in 1835, established a women's printing press and later became Printer-in-Ordinary to Queen Victoria. Like the tower of the present Victorian church, the vault was built using flints from the original church, which was demolished in 1858. Inside is a small font, and slate tablets inscribed with the Ten Commandments.

While you're there

Take a look around Reigate Castle grounds, just a few miles from Headley. The castle was built soon after the Norman Conquest, and strengthened in the 14th century. During the Civil War, it was garrisoned first by the Royalists, and then by Cromwell's supporters. After that the building gradually fell derelict, but the grounds were renovated and a mock gateway was added during the 18th century. Beneath the castle lies the mysterious Baron's Cave, carved out of the rock. No one knows exactly why the cave was built, but there's a local tradition that the barons met here while drawing up the Magna Carta in 1215.

LORD BEAVERBROOK'S CHERKLEY COURT

DISTANCE/TIME	3.2 miles (5.1km) / 1hr 30min
ASCENT/GRADIENT	456ft (139m) / ▲
PATHS	Fenced, easy-to-follow tracks around estate boundary
LANDSCAPE	Wooded, with some views across surrounding valleys
SUGGESTED MAP	AA Walker's Map 23 Guildford, Farnham & The Downs
START/FINISH	Grid reference: TQ193546
DOG FRIENDLINESS	Watch out for rabbits and deer
PARKING	Mill Way, almost opposite Nower Wood Nature Reserve
PUBLIC TOILETS	None on route

Cherkley Court began life as a kind of 'granny annexe', when the wealthy Midlands industrialist Abraham Dixon built the great house in the late 1860s as his retirement home. The Surrey countryside clearly suited him, for he lived at Cherkley until his death nearly 40 years later. Meanwhile, Cherkley's future was being played out on the far side of the Atlantic.

After making his first fortune from the cement business, Canadian-born William Maxwell Aitken shut up shop and emigrated to England in 1910. The next 12 months were a whirlwind: he was elected to Parliament, acquired a knighthood – and bought Cherkley Court. The newly knighted Sir Max Aitken probably got his first glimpse of Cherkley from one of the main carriage drives, but we must approach this private estate from a different direction.

A media hub

The outbreak of World War I did little to halt Aitken's meteoric rise. He gained control of the *Daily Express* newspaper, and subsequently founded the *Sunday Express* and bought the *London Evening Standard*. At the same time, he achieved considerable political influence. He was ennobled as Lord Beaverbrook in 1916, and served in the Cabinet during both World Wars. Throughout this time Cherkley was the focus of Beaverbrook's media empire. The news streamed into his office on ticker tape, and he was deeply involved in the day-to-day running of his newspapers. But a great country house was also an indispensable political asset. Here politicians could meet and manoeuvre, and Beaverbrook entertained lavishly, regularly welcoming famous names like Herbert Asquith, David Lloyd George and Winston Churchill. Lord Beaverbrook lived at Cherkley for more than 50 years, and died here in 1964.

A new chapter begins

In 2003, after an eight-year restoration project by the Beaverbrook Foundation, the refurbished house and gardens opened to the public. The venture proved uneconomic, however, and the estate was then acquired in 2011 by Longshot, a company which has a reputation for founding, owning and operating some of the City of London's most unusual businesses. The Grade II listed buildings have been transformed into a luxury hotel, with a spa, several restaurants and bars and a cookery school, and it also boasts the Beaverbrook Golf Club, an exclusive 18-hole golf course.

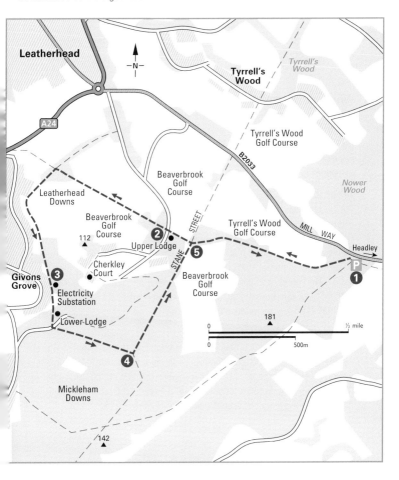

1. Two bridleways diverge from the car park in Mill Way. Take the right-hand fork, with the fence and Tyrell's Wood Golf Course on your right, and drop gently down through a tunnel of trees. Leaving views of the golf course behind, you pass a field on your left and then cross Stane Street at a four-way signpost. Keep straight on, signed to Givons Grove, and cross the drive to Cherkley Court at Upper Lodge.

2. The track narrows at the lodge and continues downhill for a further 800yds (730m). Just as the path sinks into a shallow cutting, a footpath crosses your route. There's a waymarker post here; turn left and climb gently past the houses and gardens backing onto the hedge on your right.

3. Now keep going ahead to pass Cherkley Hill electricity sub station on your left as the path drops and rounds a brick wall, then climbs steeply uphill to reach another estate drive at Lower Lodge. Cross the drive and keep going straight ahead to climb the short, steep flight of rustic steps that lead to a pleasant, gently rising path through a centuries-old thicket of yew trees.

4. The path ends at a T-junction with Stane Street. Turn left at the three-way signpost, towards Thirty Acre Barn. Follow this ancient broad gravelled path as it undulates to a crossroads with more views of the golf course to both the left and right, and the four-way signpost that you passed on your outward journey.

5. Turn right towards Mill Way and retrace your steps to the car park.

Where to eat and drink

Follow the road to Headley and you'll come to The Cock Inn, next to Headley Church, which has a traditional public bar in the original pub building. A more modern, food-orientated bar extension now forms the main entrance. It's up a steep flight of steps, but there's good access in the upper car park.

What to see

For part of this route you'll be walking along Stane Street, the great Roman highway from Chichester to London. History lies only skin-deep here, and in recent times local people have found Roman coins buried just below the surface of the track. The road was built during the 1st century AD, although its name – which simply means 'stone road' – dates only from Saxon times. You can follow Stane Street on foot for almost 3 miles (4.8km) between Juniper Hill and Thirty Acres Barn, and a similar stretch lies buried under the modern A29 at Ockley.

While you're there

Inside the 17th-century, timber-framed Hampton Cottage in Church Street, Leatherhead, you'll find a fascinating Museum of Local History. Alongside its comprehensive displays of memorabilia, maps and old photographs, the museum also features a collection of Ashtead Art Deco pottery and figurines dating from between the two World Wars.

BOX HILL TO WESTHUMBLE

DISTANCE/TIME	7 miles (11.3km) / 3hrs 15min
ASCENT/GRADIENT	1,190ft (363m) / ▲ ▲ ▲
PATHS	Woodland tracks, with two sections on minor roads, 1 stile
LANDSCAPE	Mainly wooded, but with some breathtaking views and a pretty village
SUGGESTED MAP	AA Walker's Map 23 Guildford, Farnham & The Downs
START/FINISH	Grid reference: TQ178514
DOG FRIENDLINESS	Some roadside sections and grazing animals; must be on leads on Denbies Wine Estate
PARKING	National Trust car park, Box Hill Country Park (free to NT members)
PUBLIC TOILETS	At the start

Just after leaving the car park, you'll notice a drive to a private house on your right. This is Swiss Cottage, home to John Logie Baird during the 1920s and 1930s. Baird had trained as an electrical engineer, but spent his early life on a variety of hare-brained projects that ranged from curing piles to producing jams and mango chutney. He was the archetypal absent-minded professor – scruffy, permanently short of cash, and given to sketching on restaurant tablecloths or changing his socks in public.

Baird's prototype for a mechanical television was pure Wallace and Gromit. On top of an old tea chest he set up a scanning disc cut from a hatbox, spinning on an old darning needle driven by an electric motor. There was a lamp in an empty biscuit tin and some fourpenny bull's eye lenses, all held together with sealing wax and string. But it worked, and in 1925 he unveiled his 'Televisor' at Selfridges in London. After blowing up his lodgings in Hastings, Baird moved to London, and then to Box Hill, where he continued to demonstrate inventions like the 'Noctovisor', a night-vision infra-red viewer.

Auntie takes a hand

Towards the end of 1929, Baird overcame the BBC's scepticism and began experimental transmissions under their famous 2LO call sign. It was always an uneasy relationship, with Baird continuing to promote mechanically scanned television at a time when pure electronic systems were being developed on the far side of the Atlantic. EMI launched its 'Emitron' camera in 1935, and in the following year the BBC began a new round of test transmissions from Alexandra Palace in south London. Baird and Marconi-EMI were now head to head, broadcasting from adjacent studios on alternate days. The service was officially opened using Baird's system in November 1936, transmitting two hours of programmes each day. But within three months, the Government had decided that Britain should adopt Marconi-EMI's electronic system as the new standard for television transmission. Baird was down, but not out. In the years before his death in 1946, he continued to experiment with big-screen television for cinemas, as well as colour and stereoscopic television, and Baird is generally remembered as a pioneer in British television.

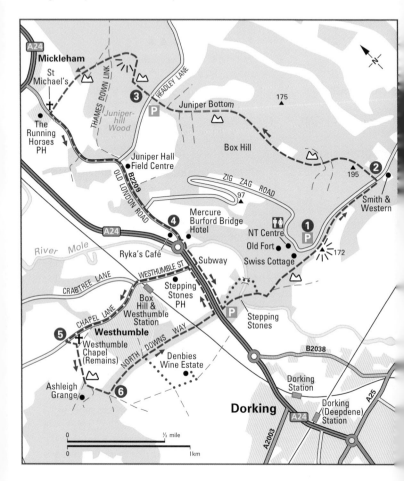

1. With your back to the visitor centre, turn right along the road to the viewpoint. Leave the viewpoint via the path to the left and follow the North Downs Way (NDW) signpost, the path running parallel with the road.

2. Continue until you reach the car park of the Smith and Western Bar, Grill and Diner and turn left to cross the road and turn left onto the signposted public bridleway. Follow the signposted route to a five-way junction and keep going straight ahead (third turning). The path descends to the valley bottom and emerges from woodland and then through the grasslands of Juniper Bottom to Headley Lane via a gate.

3. Cross straight over onto the public footpath and climb up a long flight of unrelentingly steep rustic steps. Just beyond the top of the steps, the path

bears right and the gradient eases slightly. Soon you will come to a bench seat. Now follow the National Trust's Box Hill Hike waymarks, through a yew wood, as you bear left and left again at the next waymark signpost. Drop down over a footpath crossroads, still following Box Hill Hike signs, and walk alongside a paddock en route to a stile. Cross the stile at the foot of the hill, and continue past the church into Mickleham. Turn left and follow the Old London Road. There's a pavement on the right-hand side to begin with, which at times transforms into a rural path running a few paces from the road. Before reaching the junction with the Zig Zag Road, it's a pavement again.

4. Continue past Ryka's Café and the Burford Bridge Hotel, cross over the river and alongside the A24 and through the subway. Turn left then right into Westhumble Street, and carry on over the railway bridge into Chapel Lane. Keep left of Camilla Drive and continue ahead. Beyond the houses, look out for the ruins of Westhumble Chapel on your left.

5. Immediately beyond the chapel, turn left up the bridleway towards Ashleigh Grange. Climb steadily on a tarmac drive to a line of electricity pylons and follow the drive as it swings to the left. After 80yds (73m), fork left onto the waymarked path and continue for a further 100yds (91m).

6. Now turn left onto the North Downs Way National Trail. After 400yds (364m), you reach a crossroads of paths, signed to Dorking on the right. You can visit Denbies Wine Estate by turning right here and following the path to the main winery building. Otherwise keep straight on through a gate and under the railway, and pass through large gates to the A24. Turn left and cross the A24 via the subway used earlier in the walk. Emerging from the subway, turn right and walk alongside the A24 to the Stepping Stones car park. Walk through the car park, and cross the River Mole via the stepping stones. Alternatively, there's a footbridge 100yds (91m) upstream. From here, there's only one way to go – the North Downs Way hurls itself at Box Hill, up flight after flight of unremitting rustic steps. Swing right at the top of the steps and climb gently for another 200yds (182m) to the viewpoint. Turn hard left here, and double back for the last 150yds (137m) to the car park.

Where to eat and drink

You'll find a good range of hot and cold drinks, snacks and ices at the open-air National Trust server at the start of this walk. There are benches and picnic tables here too. In Mickleham village, walkers are warmly welcomed at the 16th-century Running Horses. If you like fast food, then head to Ryka's Café, just off the Burford Bridge roundabout, which serves all-day breakfasts and hot and cold drinks.

What to see

The overgrown ruins of Westhumble Chapel look like one of those romantic, early-Victorian watercolours. The little flint-built chapel was founded in the late 12th century for worshippers who couldn't cross the river to Mickleham Church. It's been ruined for over 500 years, and only the gable walls at the east and west ends now survive to any height. The building was given to the National Trust in 1937.

A STROLL AROUND DORKING

DISTANCE/TIME	2.9 miles (4.7km) / 1hr 30min
ASCENT/GRADIENT	377ft (115m) / ▲
PATHS	Mainly paved streets, with easy section of woodland paths
LANDSCAPE	Woodland scenery, parkland and busy town centre
SUGGESTED MAP	AA Walker's Map 23 Guildford, Farnham & The Downs
START/FINISH	Grid reference: TQ171497
DOG FRIENDLINESS	Not what most dogs think of as a great day out
PARKING	Reigate Road pay-and-display car park (near Dorking Sports Centre)
PUBLIC TOILETS	South Street or behind St Martin's Walk precinct

Nestling in the Surrey Hills, a stone's throw from Box Hill, you'll find the historic and attractive market town of Dorking. Progress has happened here, but it has happened sympathetically. Old architecture blends with the new, while behind the busy shopping streets the peaceful river threads its way quietly through the town. A few minutes walk away lies Cotmandene, a wide, open area with views of Box Hill and the North Downs. Cottagers once grazed their animals here, and local people still exercise their right to dry washing on a cluster of metal poles on the green. It is claimed that one of the first cricket matches in England took place here.

Founded as a staging post on Stane Street, the Roman road between London and Chichester, Dorking later appeared as the Manor of Dorchinges in the Domesday Book; its assets were listed as 'one church, three mills worth 15s 4d, 16 ploughs, 3 acres [1.2ha] of meadow, woodland, and herbage for 88 hogs'. Subsequent lords of the manor included the Dukes of Norfolk, who lived in Dorking until they moved to Arundel – one of them is buried in Dorking churchyard. Surrounded by fertile farmland, the town quickly established itself as a prosperous agricultural and market town. The town's posterity was assured with the construction of a turnpike road in 1750, which made Dorking a staging post on the route to Brighton. The addition of a London railway line in 1867 gave rise to the abundance of well-proportioned Victorian and Edwardian buildings that you'll see around the town.

Long noted for its beauty and history, Dorking has attracted a number of esteemed writers, artists and poets. Jane Austen was a regular visitor to the area and used Box Hill as a backdrop for one of the pivotal scenes in *Emma*, while Charles Dickens is generally reckoned to have used the local coachman William Broad as the model for a character in *The Pickwick Papers*. Composer Ralph Vaughan Williams (1872–1958) spent much of his childhood in the area and you'll find a sculpture of him outside Dorking Halls at the start of the walk.

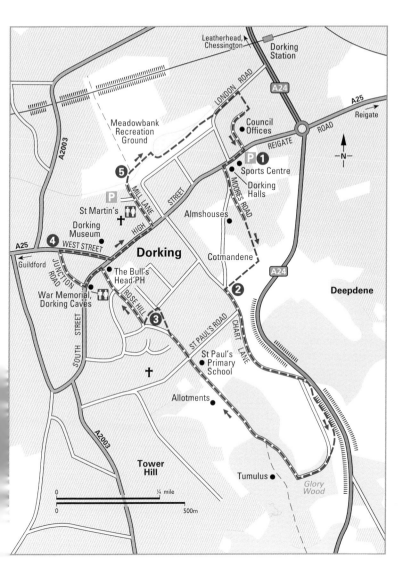

1. From the car park turn left along Reigate Road, pass the Dorking Halls and turn left into Moores Road. Walk to the end of Moores Road, passing the Victorian almshouses on your right as you reach the large expanse of common land known as Cotmandene. Walk ahead to the trees and bear right following the edge of the green to reach Chart Lane.

2. Turn left and follow the pavement as far as the A24, then carefully cross Chart Lane and bear right into Glory Wood, using the signed footpath off the verge. As the footpath climbs away from the road, steer as right as you can, keeping the edge of the wood in view on your right. Leave the woods at the barrier near an information board and fork right. There's a bench here, and a fine view towards Ranmore Church spire in the woods on the horizon. Drop down past the allotments and then St Paul's Primary School, cross St Paul's

Road, and dive down the little fenced footpath opposite. Keep straight on into Chequers Place; then, after 70yds (64m), turn off down a narrow alley on your left, signed Rose Hill.

3. Emerge in Rose Hill – almost as pretty as its name – and turn right to walk down beside the green, and then out into South Street through the mock-Tudor Rose Hill Arch at the foot of the hill. On your right is The Bull's Head. Turn left and walk round to the war memorial opposite Waitrose. Just to the left of the memorial you'll see the little blue door at the entrance to Dorking Caves (currently closed to visitors). Cross at the traffic lights and turn left and then right into Junction Road.

4. At the bottom, turn right into West Street, pass Dorking Museum, and continue into the High Street. If you wander left down the alley next to Barclays Bank you'll find St Martin's Church, designed by Henry Woodyer and completed in 1877. The flintwork alone is worth a look. Inside, it positively oozes with high Victorian art. Further up the High Street, pass St Martin's Walk shopping precinct, and a few paces further on turn left down Mill Lane.

5. Fork right at the bottom towards the Meadowbank Recreation Ground, then turn right again beside the brook. Keep the lake on your left and follow the path to the head of the lake, then over a bridge onto a path leading to London Road. Turn left; then, after 100yds (91m), turn right up the signed footpath and follow the drive as it winds up past the Council Offices, back to Reigate Road. Cross over, back to the car park.

Where to eat and drink

There's plenty of choice in the town, but for coffee, light lunches or afternoon tea, try the airy surroundings and chic decor of the Dorking Halls café. The service is friendly, and there's an excellent menu of hot and cold snacks to choose from, as well as pastries and cakes.

What to see

Opposite the Dorking Halls take a look at the striking new statue of Thomas Cubitt. Though he began his working life as a ship's carpenter, Cubitt was a paternalistic employer who built up the leading construction business of the age with an eye on the welfare of his men. He was involved with several public health projects in London, and also supervised the building of Polesden Lacey. Late in life he completed his greatest work, designing and building Osborne House for Queen Victoria. He made his own home at Denbies, on the outskirts of Dorking, and died there in 1855.

While you're there

Spend a little more time exploring West Street, the oldest road in Dorking, which has a unique character and is famous around the globe for its antiques trade and workshops. Look out for the plaque on William Mullins' house. A shoemaker who set sail with his family for the New World on the *Mayflower* in 1620. You'll also find Dorking Museum, which occupies the old foundry site, dating to the 1820s.

AROUND HOLMWOOD COMMON

19

DISTANCE/TIME	6.4 miles (10.3km) / 3hrs
ASCENT/GRADIENT	732ft (223m) / ▲ ▲ ▲
PATHS	Forest and farm tracks, muddy in places, some minor roads
LANDSCAPE	Wooded common, with clearings and scattered houses
SUGGESTED MAP	AA Walker's Map 23 Guildford, Farnham & The Downs
START/FINISH	Grid reference: TQ183454
DOG FRIENDLINESS	Welcome on Holmwood Common, but under control across farmland
PARKING	National Trust car park at Fourwents Pond, Blackbrook Road
PUBLIC TOILETS	None on route

Visit Holmwood today and you'll find a peaceful tangle of woodland, bracken and grass, with several decent car parks and the Fourwents Pond glistening calmly in the southeast corner of the common. Pretty much what you'd expect from an area that's been in the hands of the National Trust since 1956. Nevertheless, the common has a more turbulent history than you might guess.

Tales of lawlessness

Holmwood was part of the Manor of Dorking and was held by King Harold until William took over at the time of the Norman Conquest. At that time Holmwood was something of a wasteland, and it didn't even get a mention in the Domesday Book. By the Middle Ages, squatters had built makeshift houses, grazed a few animals, and cleared the woodland for timber and fuel. The new residents also went in for sheep stealing and smuggling, as well as the more honest trade of making brooms. Smuggling remained rife well into the 18th century. Nearby Leith Hill tower was used for signalling during the 1770s, and the bootleggers also met in pubs and cottages on the common itself. The Old Nag's Head once stood on the corner of Holmwood View Road and the A24 (Point 6 on the map). Brook Lodge Farm, just up the road from Fourwents Pond, stands on the site of another smugglers' haunt: the old Bottle and Glass.

Then, in 1755, a turnpike road was built on the line of the modern A24, and up to 18 coaches a day began rolling through Holmwood. As a result, highwaymen prospered here until well into the 19th century. The American millionaire Alfred Gwynne Vanderbilt also regularly drove his coach along this stretch. He died tragically in May 1915, when the Cunard liner *Lusitania* was torpedoed by a German U-boat off the southern coast of Ireland. You can see Vanderbilt's simple granite memorial by making a short diversion along the roadside pavement from South Holmwood and crossing near the bus shelter.

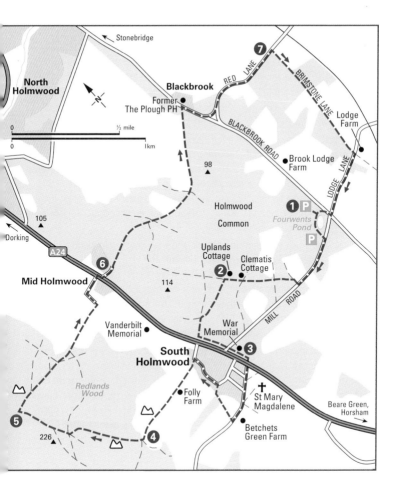

1. From the notice board in the car park, bear right to walk along the waterside path of Fourwents Pond, keeping the pond on your left. At the far corner of the pond cross a small plank bridge, walk through the smaller Fourwents Mill Road car park and turn right into Mill Road. After 400yds (366m), take the second turning right up the lane, signposted 'Gable End, Applegarth and Went Cottage'; then, 30yds (27m) further on, fork left onto the public footpath. Continue under a set of power lines, then follow the orange waymarks, signed to Viewpoint and Mill Road car park, at the parting of two rough gravel tracks bearing right. Follow the path to Clematis Cottage. Bear left, passing The Mill Cottage and Uplands Cottage.

2. Turn left on a hard track. After 300yds (274m), it swings right and comes to a crossroads. Turn left on a grassy bridleway, and continue towards the A24 until the roadside houses come into view; then bear left, and walk parallel to the main road. Continue past Mill Road to the war memorial, then cross the main road via the subway.

3. Take the quiet lane up towards Betchets Green Farm. Fork right just beyond the farm at a split in the road, and turn sharp right at the public footpath sign

75yds (69m) further on. Follow the path over a bridge into trees, and continue on the marked path into Warwick Close, and until the road ends at a public bridleway. Turn left, walk past Folly Farm, through a gate, and climb towards Redlands Wood for 450yds (411m) to reach a rough forest ride.

4. Turn right, and continue up the hill through the pine trees until the ride swings left to a five-way junction. Think of it as a mini-roundabout, and take the third exit. You'll climb briefly, before dropping to a forest crossroads.

5. Turn right, then right again after 22yds (20m) to descend steeply to a junction of tracks. Bear right following a yellow waymarker. At the bottom of the hill swing right over a brook; almost at once fork left onto a narrow footpath just inside the woodland edge. A kissing gate leads you out of the woods and across an open field to another kissing gate. Pass through the gate and continue following the track as it zig-zags left and right into Norfolk Lane, back to the A24.

6. Cross the dual carriageway with care and walk down Holmwood View Road. At the end, continue along the grassy footpath and follow this over a footbridge and then across the orange waymarked trail. When the path swerves right, jink left onto an adjoining path over another footbridge, following the yellow way-markers as it runs alongside the stream and the backs of houses and brings you out on Blackbrook Road. Turn right, then left into Red Lane (signposted towards Leigh and Brockham) and follow it for about 0.5 miles (800m).

7. Turn right into Brimstone Lane, within sight of the railway bridge, at the public bridleway signpost. Continue through a gate and follow the obvious path, passing a woodyard through a gate to walk down the right-hand side of a field, leaving at a final gate at the far end. Follow the track as far as Lodge Farm, then turn right onto Lodge Lane back to Fourwents Pond. Turn right on Blackbrook Road for the last 100yds (91m) to return to the car park.

Where to eat and drink

There's nowhere on the route, but if all you want is a quick bite on the hoof, pop into the village stores on the A24 at Beare Green, about a mile to the south. For something a bit more substantial, head for the Blu-Moon Café near the shop. Further afield, the Royal Oak at Stonebridge in North Holmwood serves real ales and well-cooked, uncomplicated pub food.

What to see

In June, July and August, watch out for white admiral butterflies feeding on bramble blossom in the woodland glades. The white admiral's wings are mainly charcoal grey, with a broad white streak running from front to back down each side.

While you're there

At nearby Dorking Museum you'll find collections of farm tools and equipment, clothing and household items, all with a local connection. There's a children's corner, and a collection of stuffed birds. Don't miss the remains of Dorking's very own dinosaur – a 10ft (3m) iguanodon tail bone.

IN AND AROUND OCKLEY VILLAGE

DISTANCE/TIME	3.2 miles (5.1km) / 1hr 45min
ASCENT/GRADIENT	253ft (77m) / ▲
PATHS	Across fields and through woodlands, can be muddy in places, 4 stiles
LANDSCAPE	Ockley is a charming village surrounded by fields and woods and close to the Vann Lake Nature Reserve
SUGGESTED MAP	AA Walker's Map 23 Guildford, Farnham & The Downs
START/FINISH	Grid reference: TQ148402
DOG FRIENDLINESS	On lead through farmland around livestock
PARKING	Short-stay parking opposite The Inn on the Green, Stane Street
PUBLIC TOILETS	None on route, nearest at Village Way car park, Cranleigh

This walk around the pretty village of Ockley has a couple of surprises that add to its interest. Firstly, however, the village itself is worth exploring.

The dead straight road that forms its setting is the inheritor of the Roman Stane Street, a road which originally ran in a direct line from London Bridge to Pulborough and then on to Chichester. A settlement has existed here since Saxon times (Ockley means 'Occa's clearing in the wood'), and there may have been a small castle here in the 12th century. The village is mentioned in the Domesday Book. St Margaret's Church dates from 1291 and the famous herbalist Nicholas Culpeper (born 1616) was the son of one of the rectors. Most of the development of the village along the road took place in the 16th century. The railway line has been in existence since 1867, and back in 1901 the train bearing the cortège of Queen Victoria passed through the station.

Local landmarks

Ockley Windmill (properly called Elmer's Windmill) was built in 1802. The windmill never actually belonged to Elmer; its name refers to the fact that during the 11th century, most of the Ockley area was owned by one Aylmer (sometimes spelled Almar or Aelmar). The windmill fell down in 1944 and, for several years, the brick base served as a store, but it is now being sensitively restored as a private dwelling. It can be seen from this walk, close to Point 3 of the route. Further along the walk is Vann Lake Nature Reserve (Point 4). Vann Lake is quite extensive (8 acres/3.2ha), and there are some spectacular views of it along the route. The lake was probably built in the 18th century and dammed to provide power for a proposed linen mill. It is now a Site of Special Scientific Interest and harbours a number of rare species. These include many species of fungi found on specially placed rotting logs, as well as over 100 different bird species and some rare insects. It is also home to dormice.

Ocklympics

The village has a great community spirit, with a lively programme of cricket matches, a superb Bonfire Night procession and an extraordinary event, the 'Ocklympics', which takes place every four years. It involves teams of villagers taking part in a variety of eccentric contests.

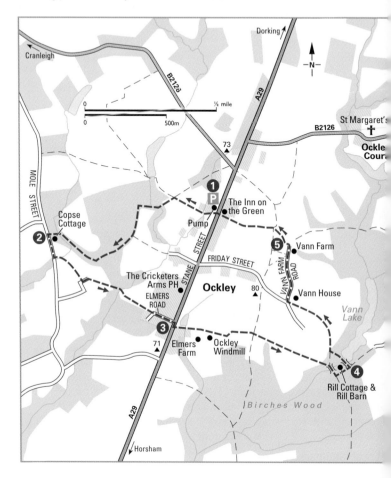

1. With your back to The Inn on the Green pub, walk across the green towards the pump and cottages, and turn left towards the pond. Turn right, following the public bridleway sign, to bear left and take the path diagonally across a field, heading towards a corner of woodland jutting into the field. Turn left into the trees; after a few paces go through a gate and over a bridge into woodland. Continue straight on along the edge of the woods, to eventually cross another bridge and pass by the side of Copse Cottage to Mole Street.

2. Turn left, pass another house and go left through a gate onto a public footpath that winds diagonally across a field towards a gap in the hedge, to the left of a large oak. Pass through and head towards a barn, then bear left and right, with the barn and farmhouse on your right. At the far end of the field, go

through a gate and down the slope and over a stream towards a fingerpost. Turn right and follow the path around the right-hand edge of the field and towards an old barn. Reach a gravel track that leads through a metal gate and into Elmers Road. Proceed ahead to the main road (Stane Street, A29).

3. Cross the road with care, and turn right then left onto a public footpath beside the gate to Elmers Farm. Go through a small gate, pass a pond on the left and head towards Ockley Windmill. Just before the gate to the windmill, the path jinks left downhill towards a stile. Over the stile continue straight on to a cross-track with a fingerpost. Continue ahead over a stile and cross the field to another stile. Again, go straight ahead across a field to a gap in the trees at the far side, and walk half right to the bottom of the next field. Cross a stile and walk into woodland. Within a few paces you reach a cross-track, where you turn right and descend to a bridge and up the stony track on the far side. Follow the left-hand public bridleway past Rill Cottage and Rill Barn on the left, to reach a footpath sign, near a wooden barrier, and turn left.

4. Descend to cross a bridge over the outlet channel for Vann Lake, and continue up to a fingerpost where you turn right. Follow the path along the top of a field to a track between houses and emerge by Vann House. Take the road straight ahead, towards Vann Farm at the end of the road.

5. Just before reaching Vann Farm, jink left and then shortly left again, and right into a field. Bear half left up a field to the edge of the woodland. Keeping the woodland to the left, walk ahead to reach a narrow alleyway on the left. This leads between houses to the main road and back to the village green.

Where to eat and drink
There are several places to eat in Ockley but two pubs close to the route of the walk are The Inn on the Green and The Cricketers Arms. Both serve excellent food and drink and The Inn on the Green also offers accommodation.

What to see
On the village green, near the start of the walk, stands an unusual monument. It is the preserved village pump, which was originally established by a village benefactor for the good of the residents. It was in continuous use until the 1950s, and was restored in 2004.

While you're there
Warnham Local Nature Reserve, just northwest of Horsham, is a good place to visit at any time of year. It has nature trails, a bird hide, boardwalks, a large mill pond and a visitor centre. It is based around Warnham Mill, which was originally involved in iron making, then in grinding corn, and today survives intact.

FRIDAY STREET AND WOTTON

DISTANCE/TIME	7 miles (11.2km) / 3hrs
ASCENT/GRADIENT	876ft (267m) / ▲ ▲ ▲
PATHS	Easily walked woodland tracks, one steep ascent and descent, 5 stiles
LANDSCAPE	Ancient landscape of thickly wooded sandstone heaths
SUGGESTED MAP	AA Walker's Map 23 Guildford, Farnham & The Downs
START/FINISH	Grid reference: TQ131432
DOG FRIENDLINESS	Can mostly run free
PARKING	National Trust Starveall Corner car park on Leith Hill Road
PUBLIC TOILETS	None on route

Somewhere in the forgotten landscape of thickly wooded sandstone heaths around Abinger Common lies Friday Street, Surrey's smallest, prettiest and most remote hamlet. Friday Street's most famous son is an enigmatic figure who blends life and legend with effortless ease. Stephen Langton was born around 1150, and orphaned by the age of ten. His parents may have come from Lincolnshire, though legend has it that he was born in Friday Street.

It's clear that Stephen was educated by monks, but although one source has him singing in the local choir, it seems that he also studied at the University of Paris. Here, it's said, he established himself as a leading theologian – a plausible tale, since Stephen went on to become Archbishop of Canterbury. By the time he was 18, Stephen was living in Albury, a few miles from Friday Street. Here he fell in love with a girl called Alice, and legend has it that the couple were strolling in the nearby woods when they were set upon by King John and his followers. John kidnapped Alice and took her off to his hunting lodge at Tangley, near Guildford. Stephen followed the trail and set fire to the house in an attempt to rescue his sweetheart, but the girl fainted or was overcome by smoke. Thinking her dead, the grief-stricken Stephen went off to become a monk.

By the dawn of the 13th century, the idle and self-centred King John was deeply unpopular. He refused to accept Stephen Langton as the Pope's choice of Archbishop of Canterbury, provoking six years of conflict with Rome and the threat of a French invasion. By 1214 the King had capitulated, but he now faced a baronial revolt. Langton stepped in as mediator – he was prominent in drafting the Magna Carta, and was among the signatories at Runnymede in 1215. Meanwhile, Alice had recovered from her ordeal and went on to become Abbess of St Catherine's in Guildford. Some years later, the couple were reunited after mass at St Martha's Church, near Guildford – but tragically, the Abbess was so overcome with emotion that she died in Stephen's arms.

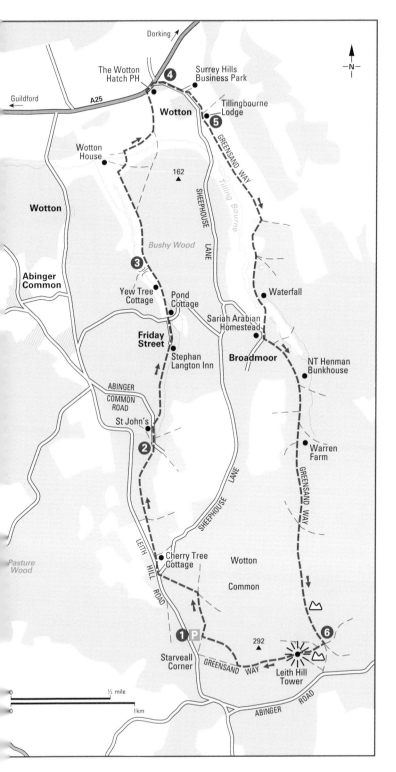

Dorking ↗

The Wotton
Hatch PH ④ Surrey Hills
Business Park

Guildford ← A25 Tillingbourne
Lodge

Wotton ⑤

Wotton
House

162 ▲

SHEEPHOUSE LANE

GREENSAND WAY

Tilling Bourne

Wotton

Bushy Wood

**Abinger
Common**

③

Yew Tree
Cottage Pond
Cottage Waterfall

Sariah Arabian
Homestead

**Friday
Street**

Stephan
Langton Inn **Broadmoor**

NT Henman
Bunkhouse

ABINGER
COMMON
ROAD

St John's

② Warren
Farm

SHEEPHOUSE LANE

GREENSAND WAY

*Pasture
Wood*

Cherry Tree
Cottage **Wotton
Common**

LEITH HILL ROAD

① P

292 ▲ ⑥

Starveall
Corner GREENSAND WAY Leith Hill
Tower

ABINGER ROAD

0 ─────── ½ mile

0 ─────── 1 km

–N–

79

1. From the car park's top left-hand corner, go through a gate signed 'Footpath to the Tower' and then shortly turn left into woodland on a signed public bridleway. At a crossroads of four bridleways, turn left and descend to a road junction. Take the road towards Abinger Common and Wotton; then, 90yds (82m) further on, turn onto the narrow, signed bridleway on your right. Cross a tarmac drive, leading to Cherry Tree Cottage and continue as it widens into a woodland ride.

2. Leave the woods and continue briefly along Abinger Common Road. A few paces after a house called St John's, fork right onto the bridleway and follow it, with a stream to your right, through to Friday Street. Pass the pub and the millpond, and drop down past the postbox at Pond Cottage on your right. Follow the rough track over a ford and towards Wotton, bear left past Yew Tree Cottage, and continue until you reach a gate and a stile, just beyond a stone bridge on the left.

3. Cross the stile and continue through the valley, past ornamental pools. The route narrows as you approach Wotton House, then swings to the right and drops down a few steps to a footpath crossroads. Keep straight on, then cross a stile and follow the field edge to a second stile. Cross the stile onto the drive to Wotton House, turn right, and climb steadily along the drive to the exit. Turn right along the grass verge of the A25 to The Wotton Hatch pub and Damphurst Lane.

4. Turn right and, after 285yds (260m), you'll reach the entrance to Surrey Hills Business Park. Turn in to the left, and follow the waymarked footpath that runs alongside the road to emerge by Tillingbourne Lodge.

5. Walk up the cottage drive, and after 40yds (37m) fork left onto the waymarked Greensand Way (GSW). At a junction, bear right on the GSW and then continue along this well-marked route to pass a waterfall and briefly meet the road at Sariah Arabian Homestead. Turn left onto a gravel track and keep right at the National Trust's Henman Bunkhouse, and right again to pass Warren Farm, where the forest road ends. Here the waymarked GSW forks right, along the narrow woodland track. Keep ahead at a broken bench and four-way signpost, climbing until you reach a barrier and five-way junction.

6. Turn right, still following the waymarked GSW to Leith Hill Tower and climb steeply as it pushes up towards the Tower. Pass the tower, and follow the signposted route back to Starveall Corner car park.

Where to eat and drink
The Stephan Langton Inn in Friday Street is a great walkers' pub serving freshly cooked food and daily specials. Tanhouse at ground level at Leith Hill Tower sells drinks and cakes as well as other snacks.

What to see
Shortly after you join the Greensand Way you'll see an impressive waterfall on your left, cascading 65ft (20m) into a pool.

While you're there
Climb the 75 spiral steps of Leith Hill Tower, built in 1766 by Richard Hull, for a view that stretches from the London Eye to the coast.

THE POLESDEN LACEY ESTATE

DISTANCE/TIME	4.4 miles (7.1km) / 2hrs 15min
ASCENT/GRADIENT	663ft (202m) / ▲
PATHS	Woodland and farm tracks
LANDSCAPE	Remote wooded valleys around Polesden Lacey Estate
SUGGESTED MAP	AA Walker's Map 23 Guildford, Farnham & The Downs
START/FINISH	Grid reference: TQ141503
DOG FRIENDLINESS	Excellent for dogs; keep on lead near sheep and cattle
PARKING	National Trust Denbies Hillside pay-and-display car park on Ranmore Common Road (free to NT members)
PUBLIC TOILETS	Toilets at Polesden Lacey (NT) for visitors only

To say that the history of Polesden Lacey is the history of the British monarchy through the early decades of the 20th century is, perhaps, overstating things. Nevertheless, in the years before World War II the royal family's footfalls often echoed within these sumptuous walls. Even if you don't step beyond Polesden Lacey's main gates, there's plenty of opportunity to see the house and grounds as you weave your way around the estate. Soon after the start of the walk you'll get a stunning panorama across the terrace and formal lawns to the colonnaded south front of the house, and you'll be glad of a pair of binoculars here. A little further on, you'll dive under the thatched bridge linking the formal gardens to the summer house and the old kitchen garden, and pass the entrance to Home Farm House. Then comes the main entrance at North Lodge, before you turn south and drop under the balustraded bridge that carries the drive from Chapel Lane.

Polesden reborn

Late in the 18th century, the dramatist Richard Brinsley Sheridan made his home at Polesden Lacey. Although he thought that it was 'the nicest place, within prudent distance of town, in England', the house was pulled down after his death. In 1823 a new Regency villa arose on the site, and this building now forms the core of the modern house. The Hon. Ronald and Mrs Greville bought Polesden Lacey in 1906, extended and remodelled the house and its grounds, and set about transforming their new home into a focus of high society.

Royal romances

The couple were not exactly without influence. King Edward VII was an intimate friend, and the cream of Edwardian aristocracy was drawn to Polesden Lacey by the stimulating company and Mrs Greville's impeccable hospitality. The royal family were frequent visitors throughout the inter-war years and the Duke and Duchess of York – later King George VI and Queen Elizabeth – came here for part of their honeymoon in 1923. Ten years later, another royal romance ended in tears. The Prince of Wales was a particular favourite of Mrs Greville's but, by the mid-1930s, his liaison with the American divorcee Mrs Wallis Simpson was causing speculation on both sides of the Atlantic. When George V died in 1936 and the new King declared his intention of marriage, it unleashed a constitutional storm that led to his abdication. Time was also running out for Polesden Lacey. Mrs Greville was ageing, and she bequeathed her home to the National Trust in 1942.

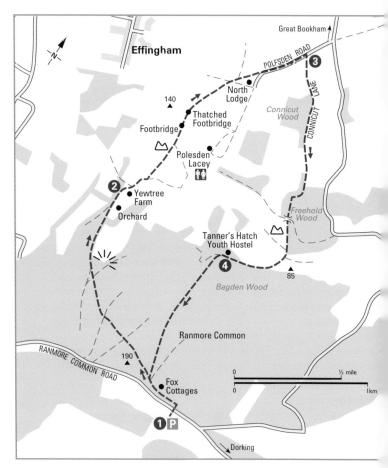

1. Cross the road from the car park, turn left and walk for 200yds (182m) along the broad roadside verge. Turn right just beyond the tile-hung Fox Cottages, where two public footpaths with metal barriers meet the road. Take the left-hand path through the woods and, ignoring all turnings, follow it down into the valley and at a T-junction turn left to pass a barrier. Cross over another track and up the other side of the valley. Just beyond a wooden gate, turn left. Continue to the gravelled forest track 100yds (91m) further on, and turn right, passing beside a metal barrier across the track. A little further on you'll pass a

bench on your left, followed by another on your right where you can enjoy a great view of Polesden Lacey, and a third bench, opposite the NT Yewtree Farm Orchard sign. Notice the massive estate water tower sticking up through the trees, just to the left of the main house.

2. Follow the gravelled track as it winds past Yewtree Farm; then, 150yds (137m) beyond the farm, fork left. Follow the signposted bridleway across a low causeway until it climbs to meet a tarmac estate road. Turn left and go under a wooden bridge, and then under a thatched timber footbridge. As you pass the entrance to Home Farm House look half left across the open field. On the far horizon you'll see a long, low white building – and on a clear day you'll be able to pick out the jets landing in front of it at Heathrow. Bear gently right past the entrance drive to Polesden Lacey, and continue on to Polesden Road. Walk right to the end of the broad, grass verge on the right-hand side of the road; then, 60yds (55m) further on, turn right down a waymarked bridleway (Connicut Lane) towards the youth hostel, Tanner's Hatch.

3. The track is relatively easy to follow. It zig-zags right and left into Freehold Wood, then dives under a stone-arched bridge. Continue down the sunken way, then keep ahead at the blue waymarker post at the bottom of the hill. Stay on this path as it bears right, to climb up through the woods to Tanner's Hatch.

4. Bear left at the youth hostel, following the NT sign for the Ranmore Common Walk, and shortly after follow the yellow-waymarked gravel track as it climbs up gently but steadily all the way back to Ranmore Common Road. Turn left for the last 200yds (182m) back to the car park.

Where to eat and drink
The Granary Café and Cowshed Coffee Shop at Polesden Lacey serve teas, coffees and light lunches, as well as a nice selection of home-made cakes and scones. Tuck yourself into a table in one of the cleverly converted horses' stalls, or sit out in the spacious courtyard.

What to see
The isolated youth hostel at Tanner's Hatch is one of the jewels in the YHA's crown. Hostellers themselves virtually rebuilt these derelict cottages during the later years of World War II, and Tanner's opened for business in September 1946. Although it was upgraded in 1998, the character of this remote hostel has changed very little, and it is still known for its regular folk music evenings around the open fire.

While you're there
You can easily include a visit to Polesden Lacey house in this walk, which passes the main entrance. The principal rooms in this magnificent mansion are the natural setting for Mrs Greville's collections of paintings, furniture, silver and porcelain, now displayed just as you'd have seen them at one of her Edwardian house parties. Outside, the formal gardens and lawns are the perfect counterpoint to your woodland walk.

A STROLL THROUGH FETCHAM AND NORBURY

DISTANCE/TIME	2.2 miles (3.5km) / 1hr
ASCENT/GRADIENT	174ft (53m) / ▲
PATHS	Generally wide, well-surfaced paths across farmland and through woodland, muddy in places
LANDSCAPE	Rolling landscape with good views to North Downs and over to Leatherhead
SUGGESTED MAP	AA Walker's Map 23 Guildford, Farnham & The Downs
START/FINISH	Grid reference: TQ151549
DOG FRIENDLINESS	Good – dogs can be off the lead for all of the walk
PARKING	Norbury Park car park, just off A246 near Fetcham (pay and display)
PUBLIC TOILETS	At Bocketts Farm

Norbury Park is a splendid area for walking and cycling. It has a variety of different landscapes from downland to woodland and farmland. Consequently it supports a variety of wildlife, including orchids and grassland flowers which attract many butterflies including fritillaries, the common blue and the marbled white. It is a Site of Special Scientific Interest (SSSI) and also a working estate with a sawmill that produces a variety of furniture, picnic tables and signs, and a farm that makes a delicious blue cheese. Druid's Grove, which lies to the south of this walk, contains many ancient yew trees.

House parties

The house at the heart of the park is privately owned. The manor of Norbury Park was mentioned in the Domesday Book, but the present house was built in 1774 by William Lock, an art critic. He restored the house in splendid style, which attracted comment in fashionable circles. He entertained many of the major figures of his day, including Dr Johnson and Sir Joshua Reynolds. Lock's hospitality was so well known that, after the French Revolution, many French noblemen came to exile in England and were entertained at Norbury. Among them were Talleyrand and a certain General D'Arblay.

Tales of love and marriage

One of the other visitors at the time was the writer Fanny Burney, who lived nearby. Burney and General D'Arblay fell in love and married, even though they were both very poor. To help them out, William Lock gave them some of his land in West Humble to build a small house.

A more recent resident of the manor house was Marie Stopes, the early advocate of birth control, who set up clinics across the country for women. She lived here from 1938 for 20 years. The house is not open to the public.

Great Bookham and Polesden Lacey

The built-up area near the car park is Great Bookham, which has been a settlement since Saxon times, and is now almost part of Leatherhead. In 1814 Jane Austen stayed in the village, writing her novel, *Emma*. The author was clearly much influenced by the countryside around, since the picnic outing to Box Hill described in the book reflects the area so closely.

The area is also the location of Polesden Lacey, a magnificent country house with beautiful grounds. One of its owners was the playwright, Richard Sheridan, who gave extravagant parties there. Polesden Lacey was redesigned in its present form in 1906–09 by the Hon. Mrs Ronald Greville, a great society hostess. She filled the house with fine furniture, art and antiques and held lavish house parties there. Edward VII thought she was the 'hostess with the mostest'; she was a great friend of Queen Mary (the consort of George V) and of Queen Elizabeth, the Queen Mother, who spent part of her honeymoon at the house. If you have time for visit before or after your walk, the house is worth a visit, as it recaptures some of the luxurious atmosphere of the era.

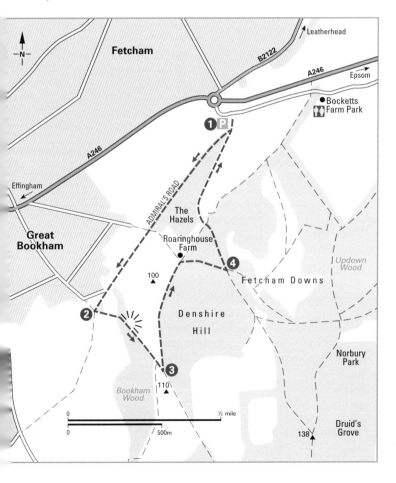

1. Leave the car park on the gravel track in the southeast corner, passing an information board. At the fingerpost, fork right onto a path, Admiral's Road, in the trees, with an open field to your right. At a crossroads of paths continue ahead, and pass a large open field on the left and then at the next fingerpost turn left into the woods, through a wooden barrier.

2. After 125yds (114m) pass by a wooden barrier and turn left, passing a seat. There are views of Fetcham Downs and the London skyline to the left. Pass another seat and at the fork in the tracks keep left. Continue ahead and when the track meets two other tracks at a triangular green turn left and then left again to walk alongside the woodland.

3. Continue ahead for 600yds (549m) as the track leads around the wooded Denshire Hill, with a field on the left. At Roaringhouse Farm take the narrow track on the right opposite the farmhouse, to the right of the small wooden barn, and walk uphill through the woods. At the first junction with cross-tracks keep ahead, then descend the hill to meet a broad forest track.

4. At this point turn left and continue until you meet a cross-track, where you continue straight ahead. With woodland to the left and an open field to the right, there are views of Leatherhead in the distance. At the next junction with Admiral's Road on the left, go straight ahead to return to the car park.

Where to eat and drink

It is a short walk from the car park along the track signed to Bocketts Farm Park, where a variety of snacks, drinks and more substantial refreshments are available at the 18th-century Old Barn Tearooms or the more recent Cow Shed coffee bar. (It is not necessary to buy admission to the farm in order to use the tearoom.)

What to see

The walk takes place in the Norbury Park Nature Reserve, which is an area of woodland, grassland and farmland. It is rich in wildlife, so watch out for signs of badgers, foxes and roe deer, and for woodpeckers, of which all three types (greater spotted, lesser spotted and green) can be seen here.

While you're there

Leatherhead is described as the 'gateway to the Surrey Hills' and has plenty to offer in the way of shops, cafés, galleries and a theatre. Its Church of St Mary and St Nicholas has an eclectic mix of architectural styles dating from the 11th century. For details of town and riverside trails visit the Help Shop on the High Street, where you'll find helpful staff and a comprehensive range of leaflets.

A LOOP AROUND ESHER COMMON

DISTANCE/TIME	2.2 miles (3.6km) / 1hr 30min
ASCENT/GRADIENT	102ft (31m) / Negligible
PATHS	Generally clear paths with signposts
LANDSCAPE	Heathland
SUGGESTED MAP	OS Explorer 161 London South
START/FINISH	Grid reference: TQ140625
DOG FRIENDLINESS	Dogs should be under control
PARKING	Copsem Lane car park
PUBLIC TOILETS	None on route

Esher Common is an area of mixed woodland and heathland and was designated as a Site of Special Scientific Interest in 1955. It also has areas of marsh, bog and open water, so a wide range of different habitats can be found here. At one time there was plenty of grazing on the common, but this has not happened for some time, so some of the heathland has turned to scrub.

Flora and fauna

However, a wide variety of unusual insects have been found, including the white-letter hairstreak butterfly, the brilliant emerald dragonfly and the small red damselfly. Altogether around 2,000 insects have been identified here, including 24 different species of dragonfly. Among the birds to be seen in the area are the goldcrest, nuthatch, sparrowhawk, hobby and tawny owl. There are flowers aplenty including dog's mercury, lesser celandine and round-leaved sundew, and there are glorious swathes of bluebells in the spring.

Royal connections

Esher Common provides a green lung for the nearby town, which itself is an interesting place to explore, with its many shops and restaurants. Esher is a historic town, which was mentioned in the Domesday Book and was a royal hunting ground in the time of Henry VIII. During Henry's reign, Cardinal Wolsey was held under house arrest at Esher Place. This was one of the grandest buildings of its time and its design was said to have been the inspiration for Hampton Court. It subsequently came into the family of Sir Francis Drake, but the original house has now been replaced by a more modern building, and the only relic of the original house is the 15th-century Wayneflete Tower.

The present building was constructed in the late 1890s, and still attracted royalty, in the person of Edward VII when he was Prince of Wales. Another famous visitor was Cecil Rhodes. The royal family also has other connections with Esher. Claremont House, just south of the town, was built for Clive of India, aka Major-General Robert Clive, Commander-in-Chief of British India, who established the supremacy of the East India Company in Bengal. It was later acquired by Queen Victoria and given to her son Leopold, Duke of Albany. She visited the house several times. It is now a school.

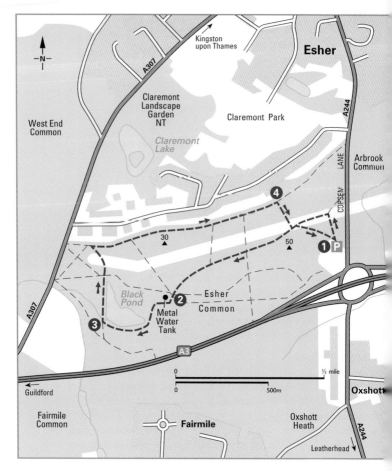

1. Facing the notice board in the car park, take the path farthest to the right, which is marked as a cycle path. After 220yds (201m), just after passing under the power lines, meet a cross-track and turn left. Continue ahead eventually bearing away from the clearing beneath the power lines and back into the trees; at a public bridleway sign carry straight on. At the next cross-tracks, continue straight on, following the public bridleway signed 'Fairmile Common'.

2. At the Five Ways junction you'll reach a notice board. Facing it, walk to its left to take the unsigned path between pine trees. Almost immediately, pass a metal water tank on the right, and 70yds (64m) beyond it you reach a wooden seat. This vantage point has splendid views across the Common. Another 25yds (23m) leads to a wooden boardwalk, after which turn right and follow the track, passing a bench and another boardwalk. Continue through a strip of heathland and eventually see views ahead of Black Pond on the right. Enter woodland and follow the path over a bridge to a seat, facing the pond. Cross a plank bridge and follow the path by the edge of the pond.

3. Meet a cross-track and turn right along the edge of the pond. From here, there are good views across the water, with its varied wildlife. Follow the Easy Access Trail along the side of the pond and then zig-zag round wooden barriers. Keep ahead, ignoring all turnings left and right, to eventually pass under power lines and across a strip of heathland. Ignore a path coming from the right, and at the next cross-tracks, turn right signed to Copsem Lane and Arbrook Common. Continue straight ahead on the main path, with houses to the left, ignoring three paths coming in from the right (the first is waymarked with a blue arrow). At the next blue waymarker on the left, turn right, following the blue arrow.

4. Stay on the main track, pass under power lines and pass the point you forked off the main track on the way out, immediately turning left. In 15yds (14m), fork to the right and the path bears right into woodland. Follow this track to return to the car park.

Where to eat and drink

The nearest refreshments are in the pretty town of Esher, a short drive away along the A244. A number of pubs and popular restaurants can be found, both in the main street and in the area around Church Street.

What to see

About halfway round the walk, a convenient stop is Black Pond. This is an attractive place to watch the wildlife, and it has an interesting history. Up until about 300 years ago, the whole area had been a large swamp, but a dam was built in the 1700s to create a pond to supply water to the Claremont Estate. Signs of the old dam can still be seen.

While you're there

Close by is the National Trust's Claremont Landscape Garden, with its small lake, an island and a grotto, as well as many other attractive features. Among those involved in its creation were Sir John Vanbrugh, William Kent and 'Capability' Brown. Spring brings wonderful camellias, rhododendrons and azaleas, while the colours in the autumn are stunning.

EXPLORING HAMPTON COURT PARK

DISTANCE/TIME	5.2 miles (8.4km) / 1hr 45min
ASCENT/GRADIENT	75ft (23m) / Negligible
PATHS	Gravel, tarmac and riverside tracks
LANDSCAPE	Landscaped grounds of historic palace, riverside path and parkland
SUGGESTED MAP	OS Explorer 161 London South
START/FINISH	Grid reference: TQ151689
DOG FRIENDLINESS	Keep dogs on lead in palace grounds and near deer; no dogs in areas of palace gardens that require a ticket
PARKING	Car park in Hampton Court Road (fee payable)
PUBLIC TOILETS	Next to Hampton Court kitchen garden

The majority of visitors to Hampton Court come to see the state apartments of William III and Henry VIII, the Tudor kitchens and perhaps the maze and the 60 acres (24ha) of riverside gardens. Most miss the subtle doorway in the wall that looks like the opening to a secret garden. In fact it is the entrance to the most historic court in the world – the real tennis court.

Courting a historic ball game
The Royal Tennis Court at Hampton Court has serious royal connections. Henry VIII played real tennis here, as did Charles I. Cardinal Wolsey built the original real tennis court in the 1520s on the site of the present Stuart court, but it remained roofless until 1636. During World War II it was again roofless, when a bomb hit the adjacent apartments and shattered the court's windows. Apart from 'real tennis', any of the terms 'royal tennis', 'court tennis' and 'close tennis' may be used to distinguish this ancient game from the more familiar 'lawn tennis' (although that is rarely played on a lawn nowadays).

The game, from which many other ball games – such as table tennis and squash – are derived, may have been played as early as the 6th century BC. The word 'tennis' stems from the French tenez or the Anglo-French tenetz, which means 'take it', referring to what the server might call to their opponent. Although the game was originally played outside, it may have moved to an enclosed court for reasons of privacy and to avoid the filthy streets in the Middle Ages. The game was very popular in France with the aristocracy, but suffered for this association during the Revolution. After World War I, it declined in popularity in England, but it has since seen a revival. Middlesex University spent £1.5 million building a real tennis court at its Hendon campus.

The chase
If you're a real tennis novice, then the court will probably look like a cross between a badminton court and a medieval street roof. Yet it's a quirky game to watch, for the serve can be over or underarm as long as the ball bounces

at least once on the roof (known as a penthouse) and then on the floor within the service court. The rackets are shaped more like a buckled bicycle tyre than a tennis racket, but the game is fast, energetic and skilful. Although there are some similarities to lawn tennis, the main difference lies in the 'chase'. This is a complicated manoeuvre and best understood by watching players in action – it comes into play when the ball bounces twice in certain areas of the court. The world champion, Rob Fahey, admits to having been initially attracted more by the glitzy parties than the game itself, but the sport has grown in stature over past years and seems now to have the ball firmly back in its own court.

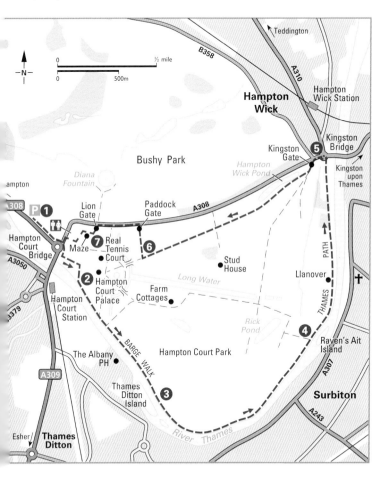

1. From the car park, follow the footpath signposted 'Hampton Court Palace' (HCP), which runs parallel to the road. Cross the road and enter HCP through the main gates. Walk along a wide drive. Just before the palace, turn right to go through a metal gate and turn left to join the riverside path.

2. Walk along the river, passing the palace and grounds that house the real tennis court building. Where the tarmac path goes left, continue ahead, following the riverside track.

3. Continue on, to pass Thames Ditton Island, with its distinctive chalet homes. Development here began in the early 20th century, and the island became particularly popular in the 1930s. Homes here are built on stilts to protect against flood damage.

4. Further on, you pass Raven's Ait Island, a tiny island in the Thames that is used as an exclusive party and wedding venue. On the opposite bank you will see the Thames Sailing Club. Now follow the riverside path for 0.75 miles (1.2km) to Kingston Bridge. This is part of the Thames Path, the long-distance footpath that stretches 184 miles (296km) from the source of the Thames in the Cotswolds almost to the sea. Turn left at the bridge to join a road leading to a roundabout.

5. Follow the railings on your left and, at a signpost 'Hampton Court Golf Club', turn left through Kingston Gate. Immediately after the cattle grid, bear right along a grassy path to the left of the boomerang-shaped Hampton Wick Pond. The path joins a long, straight path flanked by trees; follow it for about 0.75 miles (1.2km) towards the palace.

6. Before you reach the metal gate leading to the formal garden, and about halfway down the brick wall on your right, turn through Paddock Gate and follow the path to reach the road, turn left, then re-enter the palace grounds through Lion Gate.

7. Turn right around the maze and follow the wall down to a gate. Turn right into the Tiltyard; the Rose Garden is on your left. From the Tiltyard continue ahead, passing through the Kitchen Garden and then exit to the road, where you can retrace your steps back to the start.

Where to eat and drink
The Albany is a gastropub in Queens Road, Thames Ditton, 0.75 miles (1.2km) from Hampton Court Station. It is well worth the short detour because it has a prime spot, overlooking the River Thames. There are outside tables on a terrace that looks across to Hampton Court. Food includes fish and chips, pizzas and Sunday roasts, and there is also a choice of real ales.

What to see
The handsome facade of Hampton Court Palace is the nearest thing England has to Versailles, but it wasn't until Queen Victoria's reign that the gardens and maze were opened to the public. If you decide to explore the palace, allow yourself extra time. Notice, too, the topiary on the gigantic yew trees leading down towards the river.

While you're there
Visit the famous Hampton Court Maze, which was laid out in 1714. It's quite possible to wander round this for ages, but to play safe, keep to the right-hand edge going in and the left-hand one coming out. The Privy Garden has been restored with plant species from William III's day. The Great Vine, planted by 'Capability' Brown, is thought to be the world's oldest and is still producing grapes.

26 CHATLEY AND OCKHAM COMMON

DISTANCE/TIME	5.3 miles (8.6km) / 2hrs 30min
ASCENT/GRADIENT	354ft (108m) / ▲
PATHS	Field-edge paths, heathland tracks and some roads, 5 stiles
LANDSCAPE	Arable farmland and wooded heath
SUGGESTED MAP	OS Explorers 145 Guildford & Farnham & 146 Dorking, Box Hill & Reigate
START/FINISH	Grid reference: TQ107594
DOG FRIENDLINESS	Livestock in some fields, also sections of minor road and must be on leads on the heath during ground bird nesting season
PARKING	Downside Bridge, south of Cobham
PUBLIC TOILETS	None on route

In recent years, mobile phone masts have been sprinkled so liberally over the English landscape that we hardly notice them. But hidden in the trees, just yards from the growling M25, stands a communications tower quite unlike anything else you'll see. Built in 1821, Chatley Heath semaphore tower formed part of a line of hilltop stations used by the Royal Navy to signal messages between London and Portsmouth. The 13 stations were built at about 5-mile (8km) intervals, and because each one needed to be visible from its neighbours up and down the line, towers were constructed on the lower hills.

All the stations had one essential feature in common – a slotted mast with two hand-cranked semaphore arms, spelling out up to 48 different characters. On Chatley's low hill, 88 steps lead up to the roof of the five-storey tower, and the top of the mast is some 90ft (27m) from the ground. Almost two centuries ago, this was state-of-the-art technology. Skilled operators could send up to six words a minute, and a complete message could be sent from the Admiralty to Portsmouth dockyard in around a quarter of an hour. Once a day, the system was cleared for the Royal Navy's single most important piece of information – the one o'clock time signal. Before modern satellite positioning, navigators depended on an accurate chronometer to calculate their ship's position.

In 1833, a time ball was erected on the roof of the Royal Observatory at Greenwich. The ball was dropped at precisely 1pm each day and it took 23 seconds to relay the signal, by semaphore, to Portsmouth, and 22 seconds for the acknowledgement to return. The system lasted until 1847, when the Admiralty began sending signals over the London and Southampton Railway's electric telegraph. The Chatley Heath tower was used as a house until 1963, and then fell derelict. In 1989, Surrey County Council restored the shell and erected displays on the history of semaphore, together with working models showing how the system was operated. The tower is only opened to the public a few days a year.

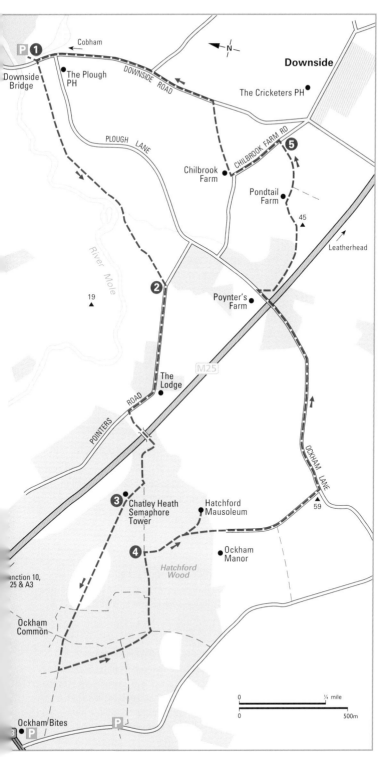

Cobham

P **1**

Downside
Bridge

The Plough
PH

DOWNSIDE ROAD

Downside

The Cricketers PH

PLOUGH LANE

CHILBROOK FARM RD

5

Chilbrook
Farm

Pondtail
Farm

▲ 45

River Mole

Leatherhead

2

Poynter's
Farm

▲ 19

M25

The
Lodge

POINTERS ROAD

3

Chatley Heath
Semaphore
Tower

Hatchford
Mausoleum

OCKHAM LANE

▲ 59

4

Hatchford
Wood

Ockham
Manor

Junction 10,
25 & A3

Ockham
Common

Ockham Bites

P

3 **P**

| 0 | | ¼ mile |
| 0 | | 500m |

1. From the car park, cross the road and take the footpath over a stile 30yds (27m) to the left, signposted as a public footpath, then diagonally cross two fields to a small footbridge and stile. Nip over and continue, to meet a metal gate on the far side of the next field. Follow the right-hand field edge, with the river just over the hedge to your right, to a footbridge close to some electricity lines. Beyond the bridge, take the path across the fields, signed 'Downside Walk'. Go over a stile and ahead to the gate and stile leading to Pointers Road.

2. Turn right into Pointers Road, and continue beyond the impressive wrought iron gates of The Lodge. Now turn left on a signed bridleway, passing a notice board 'Chatley Heath Semaphore Tower', cross the M25 and follow the tarmac lane as it winds up the hill to the semaphore tower.

3. Pass the tower and follow the waymarked route towards the blue car park, pass two bench seats, and, on reaching a crossroads with two bench seats in front of you, pass between them. At the next crossroads with a single bench, turn left onto the broad sandy track. Follow the track as it crosses the route to the red car park, climbs to the top of a gentle hill, and veers around to the left. Continue for a further 350yds (320m), as far as the three-way wooden signpost.

4. Turn right and follow the bridleway to Ockham Lane. Just before reaching the lane, at a waymarker pointing you ahead, turn left to visit the mausoleum hidden in the trees. Retrace your steps to the track and turn left, emerging onto a tarmac driveway by two large houses. Walk ahead down the driveway and turn left onto Ockham Lane. Continue along the lane until the road crosses the M25 and then, 93yds (85m) after the bridge, fork hard right on a bridleway opposite Poynter's Farm. Follow this track beside the motorway and through a wooden gate to Pondtail Farm. Bear right through a gate, following the field edge, then turn right through another gate and down the field towards the farm buildings. Turn left on meeting another path and out onto a hard-surfaced driveway to meet Chilbrook Farm Road.

5. Turn left into Chilbrook Farm Road, then turn right at the entrance to pretty Chilbrook Farm. Go through the kissing gate and take the signposted path towards Downside Road, following the field edge. At the far side of the field, pop over the stile, cross Downside Road, turn left and follow the pavement back to the car park.

Where to eat and drink

The 400-year-old Plough has a traditional wood-panelled interior and serves good food. Another good pub at Downside is The Cricketers. About halfway around you can deviate to the blue car park, where snacks are served all day at Ockham Bites.

What to see

Not far from the semaphore tower, the Hatchford Mausoleum is an eerie building. This classical 'Temple of Sleep' was built by Sir Henry Samuelson in 1921 as a memorial to his parents. The mausoleum initially contained a large copper table tomb, which had been moved from a site at Torre Cemetery, Torquay. The tomb – which weighed almost a ton – was stolen in 1961, and nature is now reclaiming the whole structure.

BAYNARDS AND THE RAILWAY CHILDREN

DISTANCE/TIME	4.3 miles (7km) / 2hrs
ASCENT/GRADIENT	174ft (53m) / ▲
PATHS	Field and forest paths, section of old railway line, 4 stiles
LANDSCAPE	Gently rolling farmland
SUGGESTED MAP	AA Walker's Map 23 Guildford, Farnham & The Downs
START/FINISH	Grid reference: TQ078349
DOG FRIENDLINESS	Lead required near livestock and in Massers Wood
PARKING	Lay-by on Cox Green Road, Baynards, by railway bridge
PUBLIC TOILETS	None on route

'*After quite a long search – walking on remote bits of line in the Home Counties and consulting Ordnance maps, we have found a country station and a line that winds through a tunnel between high wooded hills...*' Towards the end of a short feature in the *Radio Times* in March 1957, the producer Dorothea Brooking recounted the difficulties of filming Edith Nesbit's classic story, *The Railway Children*, for BBC children's television. The country station that she had found was Baynards, on the Guildford–Christ's Hospital line, where this walk begins, just north of the tunnel that was used in the eight-part serial.

Time warp

Finding a suitable location for a story set in 1906 meant 'finding a station and a bit of line that is not electrified' – not easy, even in 1957. Then there was the practical problem of the 'modern trains running their day to day schedule'. Nearly half a century later, Carlton Television had an easier job with their 2000 remake. Their film was shot on the preserved Bluebell Railway in Sussex, with a ready-made set and turn-of-the-century locomotives still in everyday use. Dorothea Brooking had no such luxury; in 1957, there wasn't a single standard-gauge heritage railway operating anywhere in this country. Looking back at the classic *Radio Times* layout with its period advertisements, it's easy to imagine a comfortable, timeless era far removed from the social pressures and changes of our own age. But in truth, these were the twilight years for Britain's rural railways. Traffic had collapsed after a strike in 1955, and within a decade the 'Beeching axe' would fall on hundreds of little stations like Baynards.

Action!

Dorothea Brooking had to cope with a different sort of twilight – filming took place in mid-February, and the schedule allowed just one extra day for the 'all too likely event of bad weather'. British Railways had arranged for a period engine and four carriages, and it was filmed pulling into the station from the

Guildford direction, stopping, and going on into the tunnel. The children in the series – played by Anneke Wills, Sandra Michaels and Cavan Kendall – were also shown exploring the station and goods shed, sitting on a piece of fence (courtesy of the BBC) and flagging down the train in the cutting. You'll see these film locations right at the start of your walk, though the tunnel is now blocked. There are good views of the station from the Downs Link – but please respect the owner's privacy.

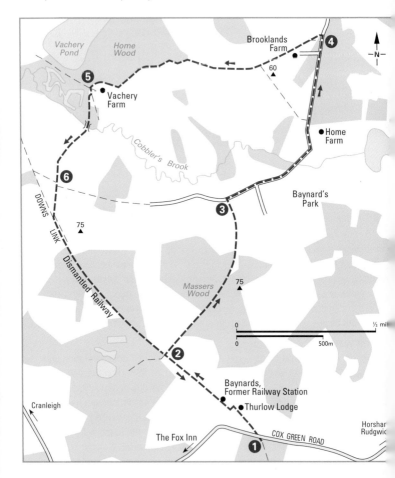

1. From the lay-by, follow the Downs Link signposts down onto the old railway line and head north under the Cox Green Road bridge. Soon you'll come to a wooden gate; pass through with the gates of Thurlow Lodge on the right. Follow the Downs Link as it zig-zags left and right, past the former Baynards station buildings (now privately owned) and back onto the old line. Continue for 350yds (320m), until a footpath crosses the line at a waymarker post.

2. Turn right here, up the steps of a public footpath, climb over the stile and cross the field straight ahead. Keep just to the left of a corner of woodland jutting out into the field, cross the broken stile in front of you, and bear gently

left along the grassy track through Massers Wood. Leave the woods at a waymarked stile and continue, following the field boundary on your right between post-and-wire fences.

3. At the top corner of the field, turn right over a stile onto the grassy bridleway. Continue along the surfaced lane at the foot of the hill, towards the large complex of buildings at Home Farm. Follow the lane as it swings left through the middle of some industrial units, and continue for 80yds (73m) beyond the entrance to Brooklands Farm on your left.

4. Turn left onto a public bridleway, which passes the back of the farm and continues as a grassy lane. At the end of the lane, carry on through two fields, following the edge of the woods on your right as far as the buildings of Vachery Farm. Bear right here, and follow the signposted bridleway until it meets the farm drive at a fork.

5. Now bear left, signposted towards Vachery Farm; then, 20yds (18m) further on, fork right onto the signposted bridleway. Bear right through a small wood, cross over the high-sided wooden footbridge over Cobbler's Brook and go through a gate. Follow the worn path across the field to a broken gate and gravel track.

6. Go through the gate and continue straight ahead along the waymarked bridleway. Follow it for 150yds (137m); then, as the bridleway bears to the left, dodge up to the right to the signpost and turn left onto the Downs Link. Follow the old railway back to Baynards Station and retrace your steps to the start.

Where to eat and drink
The Fox Inn at Rudgwick is a warm, atmospheric country pub dating from the 16th century, with an extensive menu of tasty food and award-winning ales. The pub is open daily from 12pm, and there is plenty of outside seating and a garden for fine weather.

What to see
It's ironic that the railway company's original plans didn't include a station at Baynards – yet now it's the only surviving station on the whole line. It was built in 1865 to win the support of Revd Thomas Thurlow, who had owned Baynard's Park since 1832, and at that time it was the only passing place on the single-track line. After the railway closed in 1965, the buildings fell derelict, but the complex was rescued ten years later and restored to award-winning condition. It's now a private home.

While you're there
Cranleigh Arts Centre makes a civilised antidote to a day in the country. There's a constantly changing round of daytime exhibitions in addition to music, cinema and theatre. There's also a coffee bar serving light refreshments and snacks.

THE GREENSAND RIDGE AT FARLEY HEATH

DISTANCE/TIME	5.1 miles (8.2km) / 2hrs 15min
ASCENT/GRADIENT	610ft (186m) / ▲ ▲
PATHS	Forest tracks and rutted lanes, running in water after rain
LANDSCAPE	Remote wooded hillsides, occasional farms and cottages
SUGGESTED MAP	AA Walker's Map 23 Guildford, Farnham & The Downs
START/FINISH	Grid reference: TQ051448
DOG FRIENDLINESS	Can mainly run free, lead required for roadside section
PARKING	The Hurtwood car park 8 (Roman Temple), on Farley Heath Road
PUBLIC TOILETS	None on route

High on windswept Farley Heath, you're standing close to the remains of a Romano-Celtic temple, one of the few Roman sites to have been found in Surrey. In Roman times you'd have got here along the branch road that led northwest from Stane Street – the busy London–Chichester highway – at present-day Rowhook, on the outskirts of Horsham. The Romans had a plethora of religious beliefs. They venerated Rome and the Emperor, as well as Jupiter and other Graeco-Roman gods; in far-flung outposts like Britain, they also embraced the local and pagan religions. By the 3rd and 4th centuries Christianity was gaining ground, and there was increasing interest in mystical religions like the cult of Mithras, the ancient Persian light god. Both Roman and native gods were worshipped together in Britain, and distinctive Romano-Celtic temples evolved to accommodate the various different religions. These designs consisted of a square or rectangular tower surrounded by a lean-to verandah, and they were quite unlike other buildings in the Roman landscape.

Uncovering the past

Farley's temple was typical, and you can see the outline of its foundations just a few paces north of the car park at the start of your walk. The two concentric masonry squares are a modern reconstruction, built to show the ground plan that was discovered by Martin Tupper in 1848. The temple itself was built before the end of the 1st century AD. It was enclosed within a precinct wall, or temenos, which was also located during the excavations but has since been re-buried. Tupper's finds, which included several decorated bronze strips from a priest's sceptre, are now in the British Museum. The temple was fairly isolated, although there was a Roman villa just south of Pitch Hill, some 3 miles (5km) back down the road towards Stane Street. No other permanent buildings have been found inside the temple precincts, but the site would have been the focus of regular religious rites, and possibly occasional markets or fairs as well. The temple remained in use until the end of the Roman occupation early in the 5th century, and it seems that the building burnt down some time before the year AD 450.

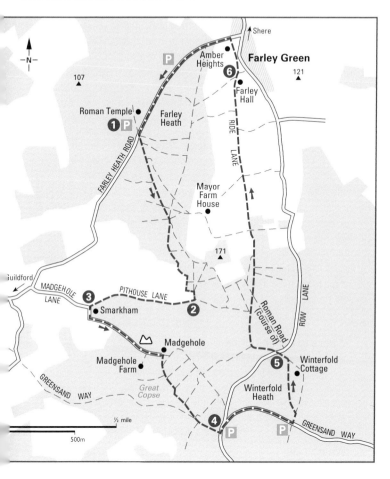

1. Stand in the car park facing the road and walk to the entrance on your right-hand side. Cross the road and follow the signposted public bridleway across Farley Heath. Keep to the right at the first fork. When you reach a cross-track beneath telephone lines, take a couple of paces to your left, then continue straight across on the bridleway. Keep straight on again at the five-way junction, and take the fork to the right a few paces further on. As the main track swings round hard to the left, continue down the woodland bridleway straight ahead. You'll wind gently down to a waymarked post beside a stile; turn right here, and follow the public bridleway for a further 70yds (64m) to a T-junction with Pithouse Lane.

2. Turn right and follow this deeply rutted sunken lane, with a newly planted conifer wood to your right. Pass beneath a wooden footbridge and finally

around a metal barrier across the track to meet a narrow tarmac road at Smarkham, a pretty tile-hung property.

3. Turn left, signed towards Winterfold, and climb through this delightful, sequestered valley past the rambling half-timbered Madgehole Farm up to Madgehole. Here you leave the tarmac and turn hard right just beyond the barn, climbing steadily past a Christmas tree plantation on your left. Follow the waymarked bridleway as it winds right then left through Great Copse. It crosses a sandy path, then joins the Greensand Way as it joins from the right.

4. Turn left onto Row Lane, and, after 150yds (137m), fork right towards Ewhurst and Shere. Follow the road until you come to car park 5 on your right. Turn left here, onto a signposted footpath into the woods. Follow the yellow arrows and keep right at the fork 90yds (82m) further on. Almost at once, bear left off the main track, up a narrow footpath by the side of a wire fence. This leads you down beside the huge garden of Winterfold Cottage to another waymarker post. Fork left and follow the public bridleway along the rough cottage drive to reach Row Lane.

5. Cross over and continue along the bridleway. After 200yds (182m), it bears hard right downhill onto Ride Lane, which will carry you all the way to Farley Green. Keep right at the junction with Pithouse Lane and trudge steadily through this rutted, prehistoric landscape until gradually the banks roll back as you approach Farley Hall.

6. Pass the half-timbered farmhouse on your right, and keep bearing left until you come to the top of the green. Bear left again, and follow Farley Heath Road back to the car park.

Where to eat and drink

You won't find any refreshment stops on this route, so pack a drink and a snack at the very least. After your walk, jump in your car and drive towards Shere. Just beyond the railway bridge you'll come to the pink-washed William IV at Little London, a 16th-century free house with flagstone floors and a huge inglenook fireplace. They serve good home-cooked food, together with a decent range of real ales.

What to see

You might see rooks foraging in the fields as you walk down Ride Lane towards Farley Green. Rooks return to established breeding sites year after year, building their large, sprawling nests in tall trees such as beech or oak. It's not unusual to find 50 or more nests in a single rookery. There's an old saying that if you see two crows, then they're actually rooks. To tell these large black birds apart, look for the rook's conspicuous bare cheeks at the base of the bill.

While you're there

After seeing the temple, you might be curious to know what a Roman priest's headdress looked like. Well, you can see one in Guildford Museum. Right next to the Castle Arch in Quarry Street you'll find Surrey's largest collection of archaeology and local history. The museum is open Monday to Saturday, and admission is free.

A NEWLANDS CORNER LOOP VIA SHERE

DISTANCE/TIME	6 miles (9.6km) / 2hrs 45min
ASCENT/GRADIENT	738ft (225m) / ▲ ▲
PATHS	Easy-to-follow tracks and paths, 1 stile
LANDSCAPE	Dramatic North Downs scenery
SUGGESTED MAP	AA Walker's Map 23 Guildford, Farnham & The Downs
START/FINISH	Grid reference: TQ043492
DOG FRIENDLINESS	Some busy road crossings; watch out for pets at Timbercroft and livestock near Albury
PARKING	Newlands Corner (pay and display)
PUBLIC TOILETS	At car park, behind visitor centre

In an extraordinary episode redolent of one of her own crime novels, Agatha Christie dominated the British papers during the first two weeks of December 1926. She never mentioned the affair in her autobiography, and the motive which fuelled 11 days of intense police and media activity has remained an enigma long after her death. Agatha Miller married Colonel Archie Christie late in 1914. After wartime service in the Royal Flying Corps, Archie returned to civilian life when their daughter was born, five years later. Agatha's first novel was published in the following year, and by the mid-1920s income from her books helped the couple to buy a home at Sunningdale in Berkshire.

Newlands Corner mystery

Material success masked fault lines in the couple's relationship, however. The war years could not have been easy, and Archie may have felt threatened by his wife's success. He found consolation – and romance – on the golf course. On Friday 3 December 1926, there was a furious row as Archie told Agatha that he would be spending the weekend with his mistress, Nancy Neele. Divorce was inevitable. That night, Agatha left her sleeping daughter and treasured dog, climbed into her bullnose Morris and disappeared into the night. The next morning the novelist's car was found abandoned by the chalk pit that you'll see in Water Lane, near the start of your walk. But Agatha Christie was gone.

While the police scoured southern England and questioned Archie on suspicion of murder, the *Daily News* offered a £100 reward for information. The story remained in the press, and on Sunday 12 December thousands of people converged on Newlands Corner to search for Agatha's body. Meanwhile, almost 24 hours after her disappearance, Agatha Christie had calmly booked into a Harrogate hotel under the assumed name of Teresa Neele. Despite the national hue and cry, ten days elapsed before the police located her. Archie was in the clear, deflecting reporters by explaining his wife had amnesia, and the couple fled to Abney Hall in Cheshire, home of Agatha's sister. This bizarre affair has been shrouded in mystery ever since.

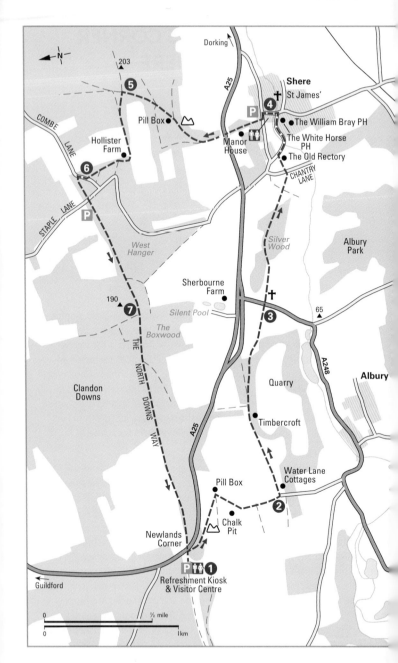

1. From the car park walk back towards the main road and turn right, 15yds (14m) from the entrance, on the waymarked byway, dropping down into the trees to a junction by a pill box. Swing right and follow the byway as it bears left past the old chalk pit where Agatha Christie's car was abandoned in 1926. Carry straight on beyond a turning on your right.

2. Turn left on to the unmarked bridleway, passing Water Lane Cottages on your right. Continue between fields to the fork at Timbercroft, and bear right onto the footpath towards the Silent Pool. Fork right again after 100yds (91m), to walk along the narrow signposted public footpath. Cross the concrete quarry access road, then continue ahead through woodland to a stile. Walk along the field edge towards the church, and pass through a kissing gate, over the stream and through a second gate to the A248.

3. Cross the road and take the footpath opposite. Go through the gate, then cross the field to a kissing gate into Silver Wood. Leave the woods at a kissing gate, turn right and follow the fence line along the next field, over a driveway, through a kissing gate and into a section of wood, and cross Chantry Lane. Follow the path beside a brick wall, and turn right at the Old Rectory. Drop down past the ford, and follow the lane beside the stream and past allotments towards the small green in Shere.

4. Turn left into Middle Street, then left again into Upper Street. A few paces further on, turn right at the driveway to The Manor House and follow the steep signposted byway under the A25. Wind past a pill box before eventually coming to a crossroads with the North Downs Way (NDW).

5. Turn left here, over a low barrier, and keep ahead to Hollister Farm. Just beyond the farm, the track swings to the right, and there are two forks within the next 200yds (182m). Keep right at both of them, continuing down the path as far as Combe Lane.

6. Turn right, then after a few paces swing off left along the NDW. Cross Staple Lane, walk through a car park, over a low barrier and continue along the level, waymarked trail, ignoring bridleways descending off to the left.

7. Continue for 300yds (273m), then keep right – following the purple arrows – as another track forks off down the hill. A mile (1.6km) of level walking leads to the A25 – cross with care to return to the car park.

Where to eat and drink
The all-year-round kiosk in Newlands Corner car park sells hot and cold drinks and snacks, including burgers, chips, soup, salad, rolls and cakes. In Shere, try The William Bray or The White Horse, both with fine menus.

What to see
At St James' Church in Shere, look for two small openings in the north wall of the chancel and a sealed archway; these are all that remain of a tiny cell. In 1329, local girl Christine Carpenter was given permission to be enclosed in this cell as an anchorite, where she could see the altar and receive Communion through the holes. She emerged briefly in 1332, but was soon placed back in on the Bishop's orders, to learn 'how nefarious was her committed sin'.

While you're there
The mysterious Silent Pool on Shere Road is worth a visit and offers another opportunity for a walk. Legend says that King John abducted a woodcutter's daughter, who was forced into the deep water and drowned, and some say that the maiden's ghost can be seen here at midnight.

PYRFORD AND THE RIVER WEY

DISTANCE/TIME	3.9 miles (6.2km) / 1hr 45min
ASCENT/GRADIENT	92ft (28m) / Negligible
PATHS	Riverside towpath, some field paths and roadside, 4 stiles
LANDSCAPE	Flat river valley with extensive water-meadows
SUGGESTED MAP	OS Explorer 145 Guildford & Farnham
START/FINISH	Grid reference: TQ039573
DOG FRIENDLINESS	Can mostly run free but on lead for roadside and golf course
PARKING	Unsurfaced car park near Newark Lock, off B367
PUBLIC TOILETS	None on route

You could hardly imagine a more romantic hideaway than Queen Elizabeth's summerhouse. This mellow, red-brick building stands two storeys high, with a first-floor entrance and a curious, ogee-pitched roof to keep off the rain. At just 14ft square, you wouldn't hold a party here, but it's a cosy enough little spot for two. You'll see it on the river bank in the grounds of Pyrford Place, half a mile (800m) south of Pyrford Lock. A blue plaque on the wall records that the poet and clergyman John Donne lived here in the early years of the 17th century – but that isn't the half of it...

Forbidden love

John Donne was born into a wealthy London family in 1572. He was educated at Oxford and Cambridge, and went on to study law and theology at the Inns of Court in London. Donne was a deeply religious young man, yet he was also passionate by nature; he had inherited a considerable fortune and he spent his money on womanising, on books, and on all the pleasures that London could offer. After his studies, Donne passed a couple of years in naval adventures to Spain and the Azores, before returning to London in 1598 to begin a promising career as secretary to Sir Thomas Egerton, Keeper of the Great Seal. In the same year he met the love of his life, Egerton's 14-year-old niece, Anne More. The couple married secretly in 1601, when Anne was just 17.

Lock up

John was in trouble – big time. Anne's father, Sir George More, had him thrown into the Fleet Prison, together with two friends who had helped to conceal the affair. Although Sir George later relented and allowed the marriage to stand, the episode had cost John his job; his own money had gone and, with a growing family to support, things were looking bleak. Luckily for the two lovers, not all of Anne's family were so prickly. Her cousin offered them shelter at Pyrford Place, where they spent the early years of their married life.

John began to earn a small income from legal work; Anne's father was reconciled and paid his daughter's dowry; and John entered the church, becoming Royal Chaplain in 1615. But just as things were improving, tragedy struck. In 1617, Anne died after giving birth to the couple's twelfth child, which was stillborn. She was only 33. John was devastated. He continued to write poetry, but sermons now took the place of love songs. In 1621, James I appointed him Dean of St Paul's, and he held the post until his death in 1631.

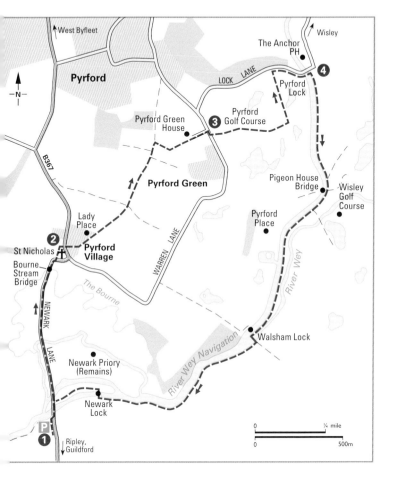

1. Walk through the car park, cross the bridge at the traffic lights and follow the roadside pavement towards PyrfordVillage. The pavement begins on the right-hand side, and crosses the water-meadows on several small bridges. There are good views of Newark Priory from this part of the walk, and in wet weather the flooded fields attract swans and other waterfowl. The pavement now switches to the left-hand side, and you cross The Bourne stream bridge; then, as the road swings hard right at Church Hill, keep straight on up the steep woodland path to St Nicholas Church.

2. Bear right past the church, cross the road and take the slab path through the new churchyard. Cross the two stiles at the far side and then go through the field to a stile on the left. Go over the stile and follow a sandy track

through the farmyard and towards the line of pylons. Bear left under the first set of power lines, following the field edge on your right. Carry straight on past the footpath turnings, right and left, and when directly under the wires turn right on a waymarked path and head towards the corner of a garden that juts out into the field. Bear slightly left here, keeping the fence on your left-hand side. Continue through a metal kissing gate at Pyrford Green House and down the gravelled drive to Warren Lane.

3. Zig-zag right and left across the road, then take the signposted footpath through a gate and up the left-hand side of an open field. Carry on through a gate and over the small footbridge straight ahead and follow the waymarked route across Pyrford Golf Course. This is an attractive place, but don't let that distract you from the golfers and the threat presented by their flying golf balls. You'll come out on Lock Lane, just by Pyrford Lock. Turn right here and walk across the bridge by The Anchor pub.

4. Turn right to join the River Wey towpath. Just past Walsham Lock, the towpath zig-zags left and right across the weir, and you continue walking with the river on your right. Cross the little footbridge at Newark Lock, where you'll get the best views of the remains of Newark Priory. From here, continue along the towpath, with the river on your left. Beyond the lock, you'll come to Newark Lane; turn left here and cross over Newark Bridge to return to the car park.

Where to eat and drink

The riverside conservatory and patio at The Anchor are popular spots to sit and watch the boats moving up and down through Pyrford Lock. You might not fall in love with the architecture of this large, 1930s building, but it's a handy halfway stop with a friendly welcome, a nice selection of bar snacks and meals, plus a traditional roast on Sundays. It's open from 10am every morning for coffee and tasty breakfast baps, and there's also a cake of the day.

What to see

This walk abounds in romance, and the forlorn remains of Newark Priory are as romantic as any Victorian watercolour. The Priory was probably founded by Augustinian canons late in the 12th century. It would have been abandoned at the Dissolution in 1536, so the buildings were almost certainly falling into ruins by the time John Donne knew them. The flint walls of the presbytery and the south transept still stand almost to their original height – but take your binoculars for a closer look, as the ruins are on private land.

While you're there

Whatever the season, you're sure to enjoy the colourful displays at the Royal Horticultural Society's Wisley Gardens – open year-round. As well as the collections of flowers, alpines, fruit and vegetables, you'll see a variety of demonstration gardens packed with practical ideas that will keep you busy long after you get home. With a restaurant, gift shop and plant centre, Wisley has something for everyone.

ALFOLD'S LOST CANAL

DISTANCE/TIME	4.7 miles (7.6km) / 2hrs
ASCENT/GRADIENT	233ft (71m) / ▲
PATHS	Former canal towpath, field and forest paths, muddy after rain
LANDSCAPE	Mainly wooded countryside, some views across farmland
SUGGESTED MAP	AA Walker's Map 23 Guildford, Farnham & The Downs
START/FINISH	Grid reference: TQ026351
DOG FRIENDLINESS	Lead required in Sidney Wood
PARKING	Sidney Wood Forestry Commission car park on Dunsfold Road, between Alfold and Dunsfold
PUBLIC TOILETS	None on route

As you amble through the depths of Sidney Wood, along the sinuous towpath of the long-abandoned Wey and Arun Junction Canal, you can hardly fail to ponder the significance of this overgrown, muddy trench. In the closing years of the 18th century, the Industrial Revolution was in full swing. The roads, such as they were, simply could not cope with carrying coal, heavy raw materials and finished goods over long distances. But in southern England there was an even more urgent imperative. France was in turmoil and the dawn of a new century found Britain engaged in the Napoleonic Wars. Coastal cargoes in the English Channel were at risk and a new route was needed between London and the South Coast.

Building the link

Traffic had flowed by river between London and Guildford since 1653, and the River Arun had been navigable to Pallingham Quay, near Pulborough, since Elizabethan times. All that was needed was a link – and it came in two parts. In 1787, the Arun Navigation was completed northwards from Pallingham Quay to Newbridge Wharf, near Billingshurst. Then, in 1813, Parliament authorised the Wey and Arun Junction Canal between Newbridge and Guildford. It opened in 1816, completing the link between London and the South Coast.

The price of coal in Guildford fell at once by more than 20 per cent, and the canal also carried chalk, timber and agricultural cargoes, reaching a peak of 23,000 tons in 1839. But change was coming, and the following year the London and Southampton Railway forged a new link to the South Coast. There was little immediate impact, but in 1865 the London, Brighton and South Coast Railway opened between Guildford and Horsham, in direct competition with the canal. Within a few years the waterway was out of business and it was abandoned in 1871, though the Arun Navigation struggled on until 1896. The canal lay derelict until, in 1970, enthusiasts established the Wey and Arun

Canal Trust to restore navigation between London and the South Coast along the waterway from Guildford to Pallingham Quay. As you'll see on your walk, they have a way to go. Since 1971, the trust has worked on more than half the route with 24 bridges, 2 aqueducts and 11 locks either restored or rebuilt.

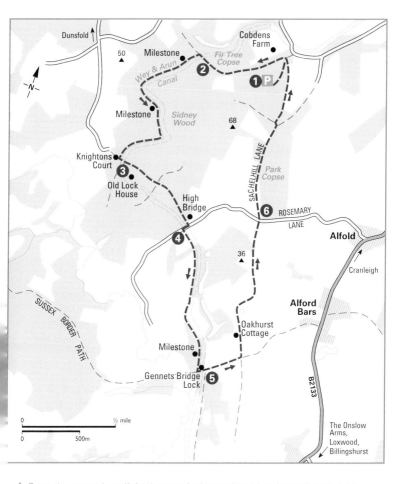

1. From the car park, walk back towards the road and, just beyond the height barrier, turn left by a short concrete post labelled 'SEEB Cables'. Walk ahead and keep right at the fork 300yds (274m) further on. Cross over a tarmac path and take a bridleway nearly opposite, and shortly reach a waymarker. Continue to follow the path signed 'Wey South Path' as it bears gently right at a fork around the edge of Fir Tree Copse.

2. Reach the line of the canal at a gate. Turn left and follow the towpath for 1 mile (1.6km). Notice the gentle slope after you pass the 'Arun 13/Wey 10' milestone, deep in Sidney Wood; it's the only clue that this section, down to Point 5, once had eight locks.

3. A gravelled track crosses the canal at Knightons Court (private). Leave the towpath here and turn left, following the waymarked route, pass a wooden

barrier and sign for Sidney Wood and then continue straight over a forest crossroads. Go past a wooden barrier, and pass High Bridge, a large white house on the left, once a lock keeper's cottage.

4. Zig-zag right and left across Rosemary Lane, and rejoin the old towpath. After 0.75 miles (1.2km) look out for the 'Arun 11.5/Wey 11.5' milestone, and continue for 150yds (137m) until the Sussex Border Path crosses the line of the canal, at the newly restored Gennets Bridge Lock.

5. Turn left and follow the Sussex Border Path for 350yds (320m) until you reach a four-way fingerpost. Turn left and follow the hedge on your right. Continue ahead to pass Oakhurst Cottage; now, follow the public bridleway signpost that points your way on a broad gravel bridleway beside several fields and through a gateway and fork right onto a gravel path leading out to Rosemary Lane.

6. Cross the lane and follow the waymarked bridleway for 0.5 miles (800m). Turn left just beyond a waymarked footpath on your right; then, just a few paces past the prominent 'Riding by permit only' sign, turn right up the waymarked footpath through the woods. Soon fork right, then continue over a stile and follow the path alongside the woodland to a broken stile. Continue on the path until it bears left and meets the car park road just beyond a waymark post. Turn left for the short distance back to your car.

Where to eat and drink

The canalside Onslow Arms at Loxwood is housed in a 17th-century, Grade II listed building and serves award-winning ales. A range of tasty, freshly cooked food is served every day from 10am, and cakes and cream teas are also available. There are two gardens, one with a play area and the other overlooking the canal.

What to see

The act establishing the Wey and Arun Junction Canal insisted that milestones must be installed every half-mile along the route so that tolls could be levied accurately. The milestones have disappeared, but the Canal Trust is installing new ones at the original locations, with a sponsorship scheme raising funds for the restoration project.

While you're there

Behind The Onslow Arms at Loxwood is a restored section of the canal where you can travel on board one of three canal boats. The Wey and Arun Canal Trust runs public trips at weekends from the end of March until the end of October (booking is advised); visit www.weyarun.org.uk for details.

BRAMLEY AND THE WEY-SOUTH PATH

DISTANCE/TIME	4.3 miles (6.9km) / 1hr 45min
ASCENT/GRADIENT	305ft (93m) / ▲ ▲
PATHS	Public footpaths and bridleways through farmland, woodland and along the Wey-South Path
LANDSCAPE	Mixture of farmland and woodland, with some good views and a disused railway
SUGGESTED MAP	AA Walker's Map 23 Guildford, Farnham & The Downs
START/FINISH	Grid reference: TQ009447
DOG FRIENDLINESS	Lead required at the start near the main road and also through farmland
PARKING	Library car park on A281 in Bramley (maximum stay 2 hours)
PUBLIC TOILETS	None on route

Bramley's big claim to fame is that it was the childhood home of the famous garden designer, Gertrude Jekyll. She was born in 1843 in London, but at the age of five she moved with her family to Bramley House, a building which is now almost completely demolished. She studied at the South Kensington School of Art, travelled widely and returned to Surrey in 1878 to live at Munstead (about 3 miles/4.8km away). In 1904, she renewed her interest in Bramley when she collaborated with her friend, Sir Edwin Lutyens, to build Millmead House, in Snowdenham Lane, where she designed the garden. The house and garden are not open to the public, but there are several gardens in this area designed by Gertrude Jekyll that open at certain times for the National Gardens Scheme. Just south of the village, Birtley House has lovely grounds and parkland, which are open for special events from time to time.

Canal and railway

The village's history goes back to Anglo-Saxon times, and it was well established by the time of the Domesday Book. Holy Trinity Church was probably first built in the 1100s, with some parts dating from the following century. Agriculture was the main occupation of the villagers, and there were also a couple of mills. One of the biggest developments affecting the village was the building of the Wey and Arun Junction Canal. The plan was to create a waterway between London and Portsmouth because shipping in the English Channel was disrupted during the Napoleonic Wars. It was built in 1816, and canal traffic reached its peak in 1839, but with the advent of the railways, the waterway was abandoned in 1871. It is currently being brought back to life with the restoration of bridges, locks and an aqueduct, as well as the dredging of the canal bed. Parts of the former canal can be seen along this walk. The old railway track has been made into a footpath and also forms part of this walk.

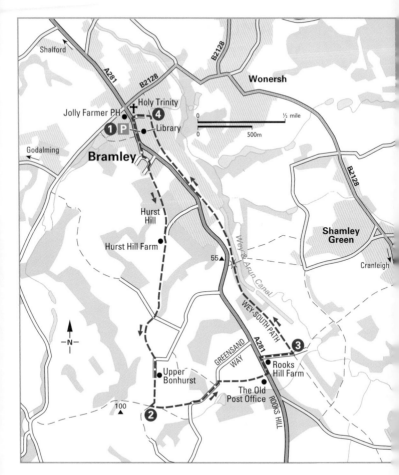

1. From the car park, cross the main road (A281) with care. Turn left and walk south on the pavement. Cross Mill Lane, pass Coronation Green with its oak tree planted in 1911 for the coronation of George V, then take the public bridleway up Woodrough Lane. Ignore the sign to the left, but cross the road and bear left through Ricardo Court to its end, to take the public bridleway directly opposite through woodland on a sunken lane up Hurst Hill. The path levels out with a field on the right. Pass an open-sided barn (Hurst Hill Farm) on your right and walk between two fields. As you enter woodland again, the path descends. Where the path divides, keep going straight ahead, with farm buildings over to your right. At Danes Hill, cross a metalled path and continue past the house. Look over the gate on the left for a wonderful view to the east. The level path becomes sunken as you start to descend and, at the far end of the woodland, take the public bridleway straight on along a gravel track, which narrows to a tree-lined path as you pass a house on the left.

2. Reach a T-junction and turn left. At the metalled road, turn left on the Greensand Way. At the sign for Brookwell Cottage, follow the public footpath over a cattle grid and through a gap beside a gate lost in the undergrowth.

This grassy fenced path leads to a main road (Rooks Hill, A281). Cross with care, turn left and, after 155yds (142m), turn right following the Greensand Way through Rooks Hill Farm.

3. Just before a brick bridge, turn left down some steep steps to reach the Wey-South Path and turn left. This long-distance path runs from near Amberley to Guildford and this particular section uses the track of the former Guildford–Horsham railway line. To the right of the path you can see the remains of the Wey and Arun Junction Canal. Continue along this path for 1.5 miles (2.6km) to return to Bramley.

4. Just after passing a Neighbourhood Watch sign on your right and before a level brick bridge, turn left down steps to reach a small path through Windrush Close (if you pass a house with ornamental gardens and a lake on the left, you've gone too far). Walk through the Close and pause in the Robertson Garden on the right at the far end. It commemorates the Robertson family, who brought electricity to the village in the 1920s. Continue to the main road and turn left to return to the car park.

Where to eat and drink

Good food and a wide variety of drinks make the Jolly Farmer an excellent choice for refreshment at the start or end of this walk. It is family owned and run and takes great pride in the provision of good-quality produce from local suppliers. It is known for a wide of range of beers, sourced from across the country.

What to see

At the start of the walk you will see a curious object on the little grassy area near the library. It is not a cider press (Bramley apples have no connection with this village) but rather a traditional Rhineland wine press, presented to the townsfolk by their twin town, Rhens, in Germany.

While you're there

Godalming Museum, on the High Street in Godalming, is housed in the oldest building in the town, a former bakery. It holds interesting collections telling the history of the area, including material about Gertrude Jekyll, the famous garden designer who lived locally. It is open Tuesday to Saturday.

AROUND HORSELL COMMON

DISTANCE/TIME	4.1 miles (6.6km) / 1hr 45min
ASCENT/GRADIENT	112ft (34m) / Negligible
PATHS	Broad, well-surfaced paths on Horsell Common, but some bridleways can be muddy
LANDSCAPE	Heathland and woodland on Horsell Common, more open across McLaren Park and Fairoaks Airport
SUGGESTED MAP	OS Explorer 160 Windsor, Weybridge & Bracknell
START/FINISH	Grid reference: TQ012604
DOG FRIENDLINESS	Dogs can run free on Horsell Common, but lead required in McLaren Park and at Fairoaks Airport
PARKING	Horsell Common car park, Shores Road (maximum stay 2 hours)
PUBLIC TOILETS	None on route; nearest at Wheatsheaf Recreation Ground, Chobham Road, Woking

The common at Horsell was originally part of Windsor Great Park – when it was known as King's Waste – and over the years it passed into private hands. The Earl of Onslow eventually leased it to the Horsell Common Preservation Trust, which later purchased the land, and it is now a Site of Special Scientific Interest. Its 855 acres (355ha) are home to many heathland birds, such as nightjars, woodlarks, Dartford warblers and grasshopper warblers. This area is one of the richest in the county for bees, wasps and ants. Around 180 species have been recorded, including some 15 types of spider-hunting wasp. Some of these bees and wasps nest in the sides of the sandpit, which the walk passes. Other insects on the common include the small silver-studded blue butterfly.

McLaren Technology Centre

On leaving Horsell Common, the walk enters McLaren Park and it is not long before the modernist form of the McLaren Technology Centre comes into view. This extraordinary building, designed by Norman Foster, is set in a delightful landscape with a large lake. It is the headquarters of the famous motor-racing team, and the building contains at its heart a huge wind tunnel. It also has a dramatic underground visitor and education centre.

The brief for the architect was that it should be so enjoyable to work there that people would not want to go home! The Technology Centre is a striking example of modern design that blends naturally with the landscape, and it has already won numerous architectural awards. The area around the building has been landscaped to make an appealing environment for workers and walkers. Extending to around 56 acres (23ha), it includes a rich wetland habitat that attracts ducks and waders, such as green sandpipers, snipe and little ringed plovers. Toads and grass snakes may also be found, and 27 species of butterfly have been recorded there.

Fairoaks Airport

Just beyond the McLaren Park is Fairoaks Airport. The walk passes close to the end of the runway, so aircraft may be low overhead. The airport was established around 1931 and was requisitioned by the Air Ministry in 1936. The control tower and other buildings were constructed the following year. It was used throughout World War II as a training base, after which it was occupied by various flying clubs. Its future is uncertain as a planning application to build 1,000 new homes on the site is under consideration.

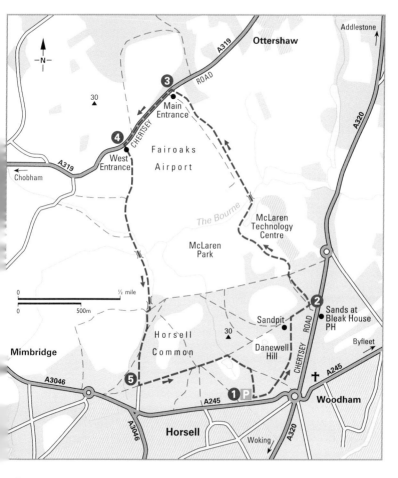

1. Facing the notice board in the car park, leave the car park via the track to the right and, on emerging from the trees, at a crossroads of paths, continue straight ahead. At a second crossroads, turn right towards a metal gate and some houses.

2. Turn left here. (To visit Sands at Bleak House turn right here and follow the gravel drive towards the A320 Chertsey Road; on meeting the road, the pub is on your right.) To continue the walk go past the houses and, as the gravel drive curves to the right, continue straight ahead along the public footpath.

On meeting a pair of cottages, pass them on your left. Leave Horsell Common and enter McLaren Park, past an information board, following a well-marked footpath. When the path forks, keep to the right. One of the McLaren buildings can be seen on the right. The path leaves the park and curves left over a wooden bridge, crossing The Bourne river, and through a gate. Go straight ahead through a small piece of woodland before the path emerges onto the small, private airfield of Fairoaks Airport. The path goes straight across the airfield, close to the runway, and light aircraft may land or take off near you. Near the windsock, where the footpath crosses a concrete track, you continue straight ahead, walking between trees. This path widens as it nears houses on the right; as Bonsey's Lane, it goes ahead to meet the A319 Chertsey Road.

3. Turn left and walk along this road until you reach Youngstroat Lane and the West Entrance to Fairoaks Airport, and turn left again.

4. This path goes past a number of small industrial units and, as the road curves to the left by the Aviation Safety Academy, bear right onto an unsigned public bridleway. The route passes between trees beside the airfield and eventually opens up to provide a view of aircraft on the left. Cross a bridge over The Bourne river and continue straight to another wooden bridge, after which the path enters the woodland of Horsell Common. On reaching Bourne Meadows House, bear right on the track, then, at a cross-track by the entrance to Norwood and Young Stroat Farms on your right, continue straight ahead and follow the hard-surfaced driveway to a car park.

5. Turn left through the car park and follow the wide path through the trees. Pass the lake on your right, then turn right and, at the next fork, take the left-hand path. Meet a compacted gravel path and turn right, back to the car park.

Where to eat and drink

Sands at Bleak House, close to Point 2 on the walk, is a smart pub, restaurant and small hotel. It serves very good food as well as a range of lighter snacks, and has friendly service. It is spaciously laid out, and there is a courtyard eating area to the rear.

What to see

The sandpit seen on the first stretch of the walk is the place where a 'meteor' lands in H G Wells' famous science-fiction story *The War of the Worlds* (1898). In the tale, this 'meteor' turns out to be a cylinder containing Martians and they subsequently rampage over much of the local area and southern England.

While you're there

The Lightbox in Woking is close by, a stimulating modern gallery with a changing programme of exhibitions. As well as varied displays of art, it hosts a museum telling the history of Woking, as well as an attractive gift shop and a good café restaurant. Entrance is free.

SURVEYING HISTORIC RUNNYMEDE

DISTANCE/TIME	2.9 miles (4.6km) / 2hrs
ASCENT/GRADIENT	407ft (124m) / ▲ ▲
PATHS	Woodland and cross-field paths, boggy in wet weather
LANDSCAPE	Wooded slopes overlooking Thames-side meadowlands
SUGGESTED MAP	OS Explorer 160 Windsor, Weybridge & Bracknell or National Trust's Trail Map (available at tea room)
START/FINISH	Grid reference: SU996732
DOG FRIENDLINESS	Not permitted in paddock behind tea room, or in Air Forces Memorial
PARKING	National Trust car park, Runnymede, (free for NT members)
PUBLIC TOILETS	At car park, also at Cooper's Hill car park

Designed by Sir Edwin Lutyens, the south pier at the entrance to Runnymede car park is inscribed with a poignant reminder that among the pretty water-meadows and rolling wooded hills, this place bore witness to a moment in time that changed the course of human history. The loss of the Battle of Bouvines in 1214, in which many English barons lost their titled possessions in Normandy, along with King John's subsequent submission to the universal rule of papacy to avoid a French invasion, as well as high taxes, all led to discontent among many of the most influential barons in the land.

In January 1215, the barons made an oath that they would 'stand fast for the liberty of the church and the realm', and demanded that King John confirm their Charter of Liberties. Lengthy negotiations began. The King desperately attempted to buy himself some time in the hope that he would receive support from the Pope. But the barons continued in their defiance and entered London on 10 June 1215. Left with no choice, King John agreed to the 'Articles of the Barons' in the meadow at Runnymede five days later. In return, the barons renewed their oaths of fealty to the King, and the document Magna Carta was created. The charter marked the foundation of civil liberty and consequently informed the constitutions of many other countries, notably the US.

The memorials

This walk makes use of the National Trust's superbly waymarked trails, before returning along the Thames Path. On the way you'll pass several memorials including one to John F Kennedy, and two very different monuments designed by Sir Edward Maufe, architect of Guildford Cathedral. The first of these, the American Bar Association Memorial, was constructed in 1957, and this simple yet effective little building is dedicated to the Magna Carta's principles of freedom, enshrined in these fields in 1215. The second is the Commonwealth

Air Forces Memorial, which is awe-inspiring in its scale. Beyond the perfectly tended gardens stands a huge white Portland stone building, opened by the Queen in October 1953. It overlooks the meadows of Runnymede where the Magna Carta was signed, and its walls record the names of more than 20,000 Commonwealth aircrew who died for those same ideals of freedom during World War II, but whose bones have no known grave.

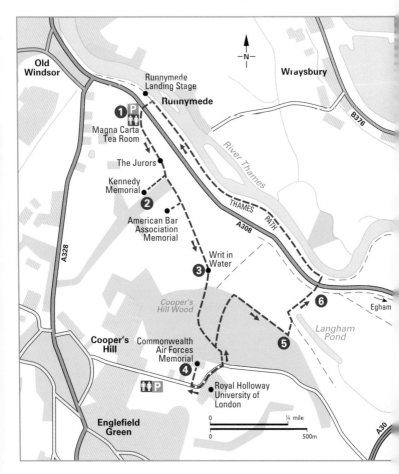

1. From the information board at the car park entrance, follow the waymarked purple route signposted towards the memorials. After reaching The Jurors, 12 inscribed bronze chairs, continue to the edge of the woods and a short diversion leads you through a gate and up a cobbled path and steps to the Kennedy Memorial. Take care if climbing in wet weather, as the granite setts can be very slippery.

2. Return to the gate and turn right. A short way further on you'll see the American Bar Association Memorial, also on your right. A few paces further on, turn right through the gate, then bear left and follow the purple marker posts beside a line of oak trees, heading towards the circular building called the Writ in Water.

3. Just beyond, pass through two kissing gates as you enter Cooper's Hill Wood, and turn half right up flight after flight of steps towards the Air Forces Memorial. At the top of the steps go through a kissing gate and turn right to walk along a gravel and then tarmac road, passing buildings of Royal Holloway, University of London, and continue round to the right to the memorial entrance. Three hundred panels stand in the cloistered quadrangle, arranged beside the tall window embrasures like pages from an open book. Each one bears over 60 names, grouped according to the year in which they died. There's a small shrine beneath the tower and, before you leave, you can lighten the mood by climbing the spiral stairs to the roof for a view over London and six counties.

4. Retrace your route past the university buildings and down the steps to a well-worn track on your right. Turn right here and follow the purple waymarked woodland path down the hill to a yellow and purple waymarker. Turn right again, now following the yellow trail just inside the woodland edge, and leave the wood via the second kissing gate on your left.

5. Continue across the meadow, heading for a gate in the copse, follow the boardwalk through the copse at the head of Langham Pond, and then head for the signpost on the road edge. At the far right-hand corner, go through two wicket gates to reach the A308.

6. Cross the A308 here, and turn left onto the Thames Path at a yellow waymark post. Follow the river all the way back to the north car park, cross the A308 again to return to the south car park and National Trust tea room where your walk began.

Where to eat and drink

You'll get a warm welcome at the Magna Carta Tea Room at the start. The menu includes hot and cold drinks, all-day breakfasts, light lunches, sandwiches, cakes and cream teas, as well as deliciously warming soups and jacket potatoes.

What to see

You're almost certain to see and hear sizable flocks of Canada geese honking in the meadows that surround Langham Pond. These large birds have unmistakable long black necks and heads, with a bold white flash extending around the cheeks and under the chin. Like swans, Canada geese pair for life, and may live for as long as 20 years. They were first brought to this country from the American colonies in the 17th century, to decorate the landscaped parks of the gentry.

While you're there

Splash out on a boat trip to complete your day on the River Thames. In summer, the replica Victorian paddler *Lucy Fisher* runs regular 45-minute trips from Runnymede landing stage, adjacent to the start of your walk. The boat also calls at Runnymede Pleasure Gardens, a pretty public park. Details of boat trips are at www.frenchbrothers.co.uk.

THE SAVILL GARDEN TO THE VALLEY GARDENS

DISTANCE/TIME	3.7 miles (5.9km) / 2hrs
ASCENT/GRADIENT	253ft (77m) / ▲ ▲
PATHS	Grassy, sandy and tarmac
LANDSCAPE	Parkland, open fields and gardens
SUGGESTED MAP	OS Explorer 160 Windsor, Weybridge & Bracknell
START/FINISH	Grid reference: SU978705
DOG FRIENDLINESS	Generally dogs are welcome off the lead, except in the Valley Gardens and on Obelisk Lawn, where notices indicate where leads are required and dog bins are provided
PARKING	Car park at The Savill Garden (pay and display)
PUBLIC TOILETS	In the Savill Building and on walk near the Plunket Memorial

The area covered on this walk, as well as Virginia Water and The Savill Garden, form part of Windsor Great Park, now called The Royal Landscape. The Obelisk, which is visible from many parts of the walk, commemorates the man who was responsible for starting the development of these beautiful gardens. Ironically, he is a man who has been widely derided as a 'butcher' of men: William, Duke of Cumberland, son of George II. He was responsible for putting down the Jacobite uprising after the Battle of Culloden with horrific cruelty. When he retired, he lived for a while at Cumberland Lodge. As Ranger of Windsor Great Park, he created an area of great beauty. Work started in 1746 when the lake at Virginia Water was first constructed, possibly using Jacobite prisoners as labour. The lake was enlarged towards the end of the 18th century and other features were added, including a waterfall and Obelisk Pond. Subsequently Queen Victoria became very fond of the area.

The Royal Landscape

Taken together, Virginia Water, the Valley Gardens and The Savill Garden comprise more than 1,000 acres (405ha), known as The Royal Landscape. The Valley Gardens were created from 1946 onwards and are thought to be the finest woodland gardens in the world. George VI and his consort Elizabeth, the Queen Mother, were closely involved in the creation of these gardens, which provided a particularly valuable green lung for people after the hardships of World War II. In spring, the many rhododendrons, azaleas, magnolias and camellias, as well as large swathes of daffodils, all provide a very colourful show. Indeed, the collection of rhododendrons is the world's largest. The Savill Garden was created in the 1930s and has had the support of royalty over the years. Originally a woodland garden, it has become an interesting selection of different, but linked gardens, with a fine collection of plants from New Zealand.

There are also seasonal gardens, a Hidden Garden, an Azalea Walk, and a remarkable Rose Garden. The Queen Elizabeth Temperate House is also a fascinating place to browse. Within Windsor Great Park, this walk and the countryside making up The Savill Garden, Virginia Water, and the Valley Gardens form one of the most enchanting areas of the county.

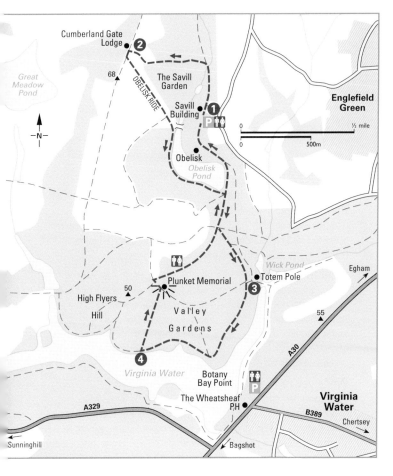

1. Facing the entrance to the Savill Building, turn right following the signpost to Deer Park, Bishops Gate and Cow Pond. Walk along a tarmac path with The Savill Garden to the left. At a fork, bear left around the perimeter of the garden and continue, ignoring side tracks, until you pass Garden House and reach Cumberland Gate Lodge to the right.

2. Turn sharp left, almost doubling back on yourself, along Obelisk Ride, a straight, wide, grassy path heading towards the Cumberland Obelisk. Just before reaching the bridge, take the path on the right alongside Obelisk Pond. Follow this track, keeping the pond on the left, to a T-junction with a tarmac path. Sit and watch the pond awhile, before turning right along the path and on to a meeting of five paths. Take the second left path, signed to the Totem Pole.

3. At the Totem Pole there are two display boards with information about the gardens. With your back to the Totem Pole and the boards, turn left, following the sign for the walk round the lake. On meeting another track, keep right and arrive at Botany Bay Point, an open grassy area on the lake edge. Continue on the left-hand track, nearest the notice board on your right, to reach the Main Valley. There are no clear landmarks, but the Main Valley can be identified by a grassy area with a single seat on the right of the path and a broad grass path leading uphill, to a small white building.

4. Turn right, off the lakeside path, and head uphill to reach the Plunket Memorial, from where there are superb views across Virginia Water. With your back to the memorial take the path to the right, which soon meets another path coming from the left. Continue right and, at a cross-track, follow the sign to The Savill Garden (not wheelchairs), and at another cross-track continue straight ahead to soon reach Obelisk Pond. Walk on with the pond on your left to reach a picnic area, children's play area and then the Obelisk itself on the left. From the Obelisk the path continues ahead to return to the car park.

Where to eat and drink

The Savill Building at the start of the walk has a coffee bar and restaurant that provide a good selection of food. There is no need to buy an entrance ticket to The Savill Garden in order to use it. The same building also houses an attractive gift shop and a small art gallery.

What to see

Around the halfway point of this walk is an extraordinary – and very tall – totem pole. It was erected in 1958 to mark the centenary of the birth of British Columbia, in Canada. It has been carved from a single red cedar and is divided into ten sections. Each section represents the mythical ancestor of a particular native clan, such as the 'man with a large hat' or 'halibut man'.

While you're there

Just down the road, near Egham, is Runnymede, a site with a great historical legacy. It is famous as the place where King John was forced by the barons to sign Magna Carta, and a domed classical temple commemorates the deed. Other memorials nearby are to John F Kennedy and to members of the Allied Air Forces who died during World War II. These are all set in a beautiful natural landscape near the River Thames.

AROUND CHOBHAM COMMON

DISTANCE/TIME	3.2 miles (5.2km) / 1hr 30min
ASCENT/GRADIENT	147ft (45m) / ▲
PATHS	Broad bridleway tracks, can be boggy in places
LANDSCAPE	Rolling heathland with some wooded areas
SUGGESTED MAP	OS Explorer 160 Windsor, Weybridge & Bracknell
START/FINISH	Grid reference: SU973649
DOG FRIENDLINESS	Keep dogs under control, especially near grazing animals
PARKING	Pay and display at Staple Hill car park, between Chobham and Longcross
PUBLIC TOILETS	None on route

There are only around 60 species of butterflies in the British Isles and you can see 29 of them on Chobham Common. The litany of flora and fauna goes on; for instance, more than 200 species of birds live in this country or visit regularly, and over 100 of them have been recorded on Chobham's lowland heaths. All this explains why Chobham Common is the largest National Nature Reserve in Southeast England, but it's also one of Europe's best protected wildlife sites.

As any estate agent will tell you, the three most important things to consider when looking for a home are location, location and location. That's true for wildlife too, and for many species heathland is the ideal home. But lowland heaths can only survive in specific places. They won't develop across most of continental Europe, with its hot summers and harsh winters – they need a more temperate climate, found around the western seaboard and on offshore islands like Britain. The geology is also an important factor, and heaths just love the acid conditions of Surrey's gravels, sands and clays.

With all this going for it, you'd guess that heathland has a pretty secure future. Unfortunately not, for this artificial habitat is the product of thousands of years of clearance, cultivation and grazing. As agriculture has intensified, traditional methods of land management have all but died out. Many acres of heathland have reverted to scrub or dense 'secondary' woodland, which has relatively little wildlife value. Conservation of the Common is mainly about preserving the open heathland vegetation. At Chobham, you might see traditional breeds of cattle grazing, and also encounter more modern methods of management, including heather cutting, tree clearance and turf stripping, replicating the traditional harvesting of building materials and fuel. The last section of the walk crosses the eastern fringe of the Common, burned in a devastating blaze in July 2013. The fire destroyed 5 acres (2ha) of habitat including territories of the rare Dartford warbler, as well as killing untold numbers of reptiles, snakes and insects. It will take time for Chobham Common to recover, but the fire demonstrates how fragile and precious this landscape is and the importance of protecting it for the future.

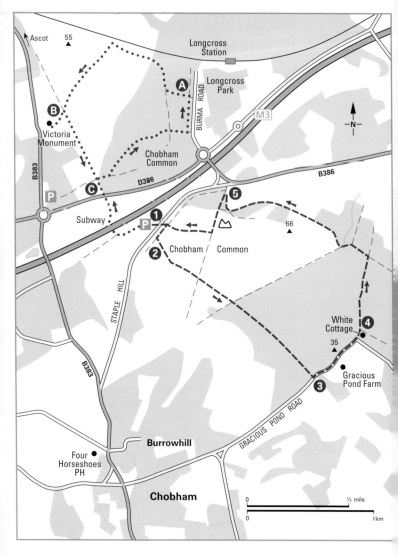

1. Cross the road from the car park and, after a few paces, turn right onto the waymarked sandy track running parallel with the road on your right.

2. In 200yds (183m), you'll near the road at a locked barrier; turn hard left here, onto the waymarked gravel/sandy track to cross the middle of the common. There are several crossroads and turnings, but keep straight ahead, passing beneath power lines, until you reach Gracious Pond Road.

3. Turn left onto the road, pass the thatched buildings of Gracious Pond Farm, and continue to the sharp right-hand bend. Keep straight on here, up the signposted footpath. After 35yds (32m), the track bends to the right; keep straight on again, plunging into the woods at a barrier gate and keeping left at the fork 50yds (46m) further on.

4. Follow the path as it climbs gently through a conifer plantation until, just beyond the power lines, another path merges from your right, bear right at a waymarker post a few paces further on. Follow the bridleway around to the left, crossing a bridge over a small stream, take the next left, following the blue waymarked route, and walk alongside a fence on your right. The path undulates and slowly bears away from the fence, until you come to a waymarker at a distorted crossroads junction. Bear right to reach another waymark post a few paces beyond a wooden sleeper causeway on your right.

5. Swing hard left here and follow the track as it bears around to the left for 60yds (54m) before getting into its stride and heading, straight as an arrow, in an obvious line across the open heath. After about 230yds (210m), take the first waymarked footpath on your right, and follow the narrow sandy path up through the gorse and over a wooden sleeper causeway. At the top of the hill, you'll recognise the wooden barrier just a few paces from the road. Cross the road back to the car park.

Extending the walk To extend your walk by 3.2 miles (5.2km), take the path at the top left-hand corner of the car park towards the M3. Follow the path, bearing right at junctions, to pass under the M3 and then bear right to the B386. Cross onto Chobham Common, then turn right on a waymarked bridleway. After a bench (right), take the left fork. The path goes straight on and then bears right, still following the blue waymakers. As the path bears right, follow it until just before reaching a road, at a bench seat turn left, and left again at the next waymarked bridleway crossroads, Point A. The track bears right past a waymark, through light woodland, then emerges to bend left, the railway line now visible to your right. Continue to an oblique bridleway crossroads and waymark post, Point B. Keep straight ahead to see the Victoria Monument, bearing right at a bench seat; otherwise bear left here and follow the bridleway to the B386, Point C, to retrace your outward steps.

Where to eat and drink
The whitewashed Four Horseshoes is set back on the green at Burrowhill and serves a variety of snacks and daily specials.

What to see
Among the many different fungi on the common in autumn, you're sure to recognise the fairytale red of the poisonous fly agaric (*Amanita muscaria*). The dome-shaped cap is the colour of tomato soup, flecked with creamy-white scales. Don't pick one!

While you're there
A short drive north from Chobham brings you to the gentle landscapes of The Savill Garden, on the southern outskirts of Windsor Great Park. Sir Eric Savill created his woodland gardens to showcase the best of every season, from springtime daffodils and azaleas right through to winter evergreens, as well as the indoor displays in the Queen Elizabeth Temperate House.

GUILDFORD TO CHILWORTH

DISTANCE/TIME	6.4 miles (10.3km) / 2hrs 45min
ASCENT/GRADIENT	965ft (294m) / ▲ ▲ ▲
PATHS	Paved streets, riverside towpath, and downland and field tracks
LANDSCAPE	Big views from Pewley Down and gentle riparian scenery
SUGGESTED MAP	AA Walker's Map 23 Guildford, Farnham & The Downs
START/FINISH	Grid reference: SU991494
DOG FRIENDLINESS	Lead required in town
PARKING	Farnham Road car park (pay and display) next to Guildford Railway Station; or Halfpenny Lane car park (start from Point 3)
PUBLIC TOILETS	At Farnham Road car park

The eldest son of a Cheshire rector, Charles Dodgson was born in 1832. He studied mathematics at Oxford, where he later became a university lecturer. Meanwhile, the family had moved to Yorkshire, and after his father's death in 1868, his sisters set their hearts on moving to Guildford. Charles bought them The Chestnuts, a large house in Castle Hill (No. 3) that you'll see on your way out of town. He spent a good deal of his own time there, too, and came to regard the place as home. He stayed at The Chestnuts every Christmas, and it was in Guildford that he began work on *The Hunting of the Snark*.

Gifted storyteller

However, Dodgson's job was in Oxford, where he was often surrounded by his colleagues' young children. He wrote them countless letters, frequently including fantastic tales illustrated with his own sketches. He was a great storyteller, too, gifted at weaving everyday events into elaborate fables while the children listened at his knee. One of those children was Alice Liddell, daughter of the Dean of Christ Church. She was just four years old when her family moved to Oxford and, with her brother and two sisters, she delighted in Dodgson's company. They would go on walks and picnics together, and of course he would tell them stories.

Begin at the beginning

But Alice was different – not content with just hearing Dodgson's stories, she begged the mathematics lecturer to write them down for her. And so, after a day out picnicking with the children on the Thames in 1862, Charles Dodgson sat down to write the manuscript of *Alice in Wonderland*. His friends eventually persuaded him to get the story published, but, when the book finally appeared with its well-known Tenniel illustrations, Dodgson's name was nowhere to be seen. Even the author, 'Lewis Carroll', was a creature of his own imagination.

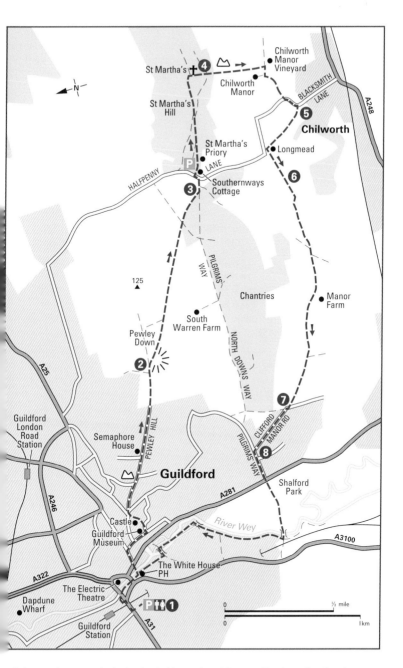

1. Leave the car park via the footbridge at Level 5, cross Farnham Road and turn right. Just beyond the railway bridge, drop into the subway on your left, and follow the signposts to the 'Town Centre via Riverside Walk'. Follow the riverside walk to The White House pub. Turn left over the bridge, continue into the High Street and turn first right into Quarry Street. Pass Guildford Museum and turn immediately left through Castle Arch. After 25yds (22m), continue ahead on the footpath running through the castle grounds, bear left around the castle and emerge onto Sydenham Road, cross over South Hill and turn right into Pewley Hill. Climb steadily past the Semaphore House on the corner of Semaphore Road. At the end of the road, continue along the bridleway, and follow it to the viewpoint pillar on the summit of Pewley Down.

2. From the viewpoint, head towards a green metal seat on your left and follow the path off the ridge, keeping the hedge on your left. Soon enter a tunnel of trees, and emerge between hedges. Keep straight on at the crossroads by the Pewley Down information board, and continue uphill for 300yds (274m) until the path meets the North Downs Way (NDW) at the blue bridleway marker.

3. Turn left onto the NDW and follow the waymarked route across Halfpenny Lane. Jink left and then right, passing Southernways Cottage on a narrow footpath, but still on the NDW. Meet the wide sandy track by St Martha's Priory and climb the sandy track signed to St Martha's Church on the summit of St Martha's Hill.

4. Turn right at the church and take the footpath leading out of the churchyard opposite the south transept. Drop steeply down to Chilworth Manor, turn right at the bottom of the hill and, a short way further on, turn left onto the manor house drive. Follow this out to a bend in Halfpenny Lane, and keep straight on to the sharp left-hand bend at Halfpenny Corner.

5. Continue straight ahead for a few paces, then fork right up the signposted path between the hedges bordering two large houses. You'll come out briefly onto Halfpenny Lane; turn left, then left again at the post box a few paces further on. Go through the gate, and follow the field edge path on your left.

6. Continue past a range of red-roofed barns, slowly being swallowed by ivy, and then to Manor Farm itself. At the farm, bear right through a signposted gap, and follow the field around to the left, with a hedge on your left and an open field on your right. Where the hedge comes to an end, veer right and follow the path across the open field. Look just to the right as you go, for a glimpse of Guildford's distinctively modern cathedral in the distance.

7. On the far side of the field, go through a gap, then turn right onto Clifford Manor Road. Follow it around to the left and, on meeting Pilgrims' Way, turn left.

8. Continue to the A281. Cross over and walk across Shalford Park, signed to 'St Catherines Chapel', heading for a gap in the trees. Beyond the trees you'll reach the River Wey; cross the footbridge, and follow the towpath towards Guildford, with the river on your right. After passing over a small bridge and sluice, bear left across the green and cross another bridge and sluice before reaching the lattice girder footbridge at Millmead Lock. Cross the bridge and continue past the Alice statue on the little green near The White House pub. Follow the riverbank until you reach the 1913 Electricity Works (now the Electric Theatre) on the opposite bank. Turn left, climb the steps, and retrace your route through the subway to the car park.

Where to eat and drink

Guildford's lively town centre will spoil you for choice. If you fancy a pub lunch, relax in The King's Head's flower-filled courtyard or try The Britannia, The White House or the George Abbot, all near the river. For virtually any other type of cuisine, head into the shopping centre, where a number of popular restaurant chains are well represented and there are also plenty of small and friendly family-run eateries to tempt you.

What to see

The remote Norman Church of St Martha stands on the Pilgrims' Way, about 0.5 miles (800m) from the nearest road. There's been a church here for more than 1,000 years, although the building you'll see now was extensively restored by Henry Woodyer in 1846–50, following one of the alarmingly frequent explosions at Chilworth gunpowder mills at the foot of the hill. The little cruciform building, which looks like a miniature-sized cathedral, is still used for regular Sunday worship, and the views from the top are outstanding.

While you're there

Don't leave Guildford without making a trip to Dapdune Wharf, formerly the barge-building site for the River Wey Navigation, and now the National Trust's visitor centre. Here you'll find the restored oak-constructed Wey barge *Reliance* exhibited in a dry berth, together with interactive displays telling the story of one of the oldest river navigations in the country.

A CIRCUIT AROUND CATTESHALL

DISTANCE/TIME	3.9 miles (6.4km) / 2hrs
ASCENT/GRADIENT	577ft (176m) / ▲
PATHS	Several paths are well surfaced, others are through woods and farmland, 5 stiles
LANDSCAPE	Rising above Catteshall there are good views of Farncombe and, later, of attractive farmland
SUGGESTED MAP	AA Walker's Map 23 Guildford, Farnham & The Downs
START/FINISH	Grid reference: SU981445
DOG FRIENDLINESS	Generally good, but on lead near livestock
PARKING	On Catteshall Road near the lock
PUBLIC TOILETS	In Farnham Boat House at Catteshall Lock

The stretch of water between Godalming and Guildford was described by William Cobbett as 'the prettiest four miles in all England'. The starting point of this walk, Catteshall, is on the riverbank and full of interest. Catteshall Bridge is built on the piers of a medieval bridge that crossed the millstream. The mill itself, listed in the Domesday Book, is now converted into housing. It was once used for making paper, although in its time it also ground corn, made leather and was a fulling mill for the processing of cloth. In its paper-making days the mill used a Fourneyron water turbine, which was the largest of its type ever made. This turbine is of such historic interest that it is now in the Ironbridge Gorge Museum in Shropshire. To the west of the lock at Catteshall lies a water-meadow known as the Lammas Lands. The name comes from the festival of Lammas ('loaf mass') on 1 August when, after the hay had been gathered, a loaf was baked and consecrated to celebrate the harvest. It is now a Site of Nature Conservation Interest.

Titanic hero

The nearby town of Farncombe also has an interesting history. It was the site of the first camp of the Boy Scouts, organised by Baden-Powell. St John's Church has a tablet on its wall that commemorates Jack Phillips, once a chorister at the church here. Phillips later became the senior wireless operator on RMS *Titanic*. He continued working as the ship sank, trying to contact other vessels to come to the rescue. He is also commemorated by a memorial garden in Godalming and by a pub in Godalming that is named after him.

Godalming Navigation

The waterway that forms the start of the walk is known as the Godalming Navigation. It was opened in 1764 to extend the Wey Navigation from Guildford to Godalming. The first bridge you encounter along the walk is Trowers Bridge (originally known as Perry Bridge, after the local architect, John Perry, who designed the bridge, as well as The Pepperpot in the centre of Godalming).

To the left, just before the bridge, are the Wyatt Almshouses, of which only the chimneys are visible. These were built in 1622 for 'ten poor men of deserving character,' and more recently some additional dwellings have been constructed. They are an interesting site to explore at the end of the walk.

After leaving the canal towpath, the walk climbs towards Farley Hill and Unsted Wood, and loops round through farmland back into Catteshall.

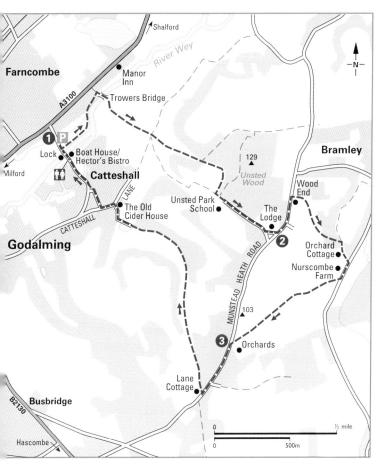

1. Start at the bridge over the river and walk to the bank opposite Farnham Boat House. Go along the towpath away from the road bridge to Trowers Bridge. (To visit the Manor Inn continue ahead for 125yds/114m.) To continue the walk, turn right over the bridge and go straight ahead, ignoring the public bridleway on the left. At the next waymarked cross-track a few paces on, take the left-hand bridleway as it runs alongside a sloping paddock. Near the top of the paddock, pass beneath a large fallen tree, and at a junction of paths keep ahead on a slow and steady ascent on the sunken path. At the top, continue ahead, walking alongside a high metal fence behind which is Unsted Park School. Turn left along the tarmac drive and then bear left at the bottom, past The Lodge, to Munstead Heath Road.

2. Turn left along the road, passing Munstead View Road and downhill until, at a concealed sign by Wood End, turn right along a public bridleway that emerges onto a gravel driveway by Orchard Cottage. Turn left, and, at the road, turn right by Nursecombe Cottages. Pass a small pond on the left, and turn right just beyond Nursecombe Farm, along a public footpath. This bears left over a stile and uphill, keeping to the left of the field. Go over another stile and follow the path between fields and, after a third stile, along an avenue of coppiced hazel. After a couple more stiles, you walk along a wider track past a house, Orchards, with a large stone wall on the left (private).

3. At the road, turn left and continue ahead. Turn right along a public bridleway that descends and eventually passes the entrance to Catteshall Farm. The path becomes tarmac and heads towards several properties. At a T-junction by The Old Cider House, turn left along Catteshall Lane, and then turn right down Catteshall Road. Cross Warramill Road, Brock's Close and then Lammas Road. The road passes over the River Wey, and you continue along the main road to return to the Boat House.

Where to eat and drink

The Manor (Beefeater) Inn, a short distance from the walk, near Trowers Bridge, is a convenient place for refreshment. It is a welcoming pub, with a good selection of reasonably priced food and drink to suit most tastes. It also has a large garden that runs down to the riverside path. Hector's Bistro in the Boat House also provides nourishing fare.

What to see

The walk passes close to Unsted Park, an elegant house built between 1786 and 1796. It was built for Thomas Parry, one of the Commissioners of the Godalming Navigation. The house was subsequently bought by Captain Albemarle Bertie, who had been a captain at the Battle of the Glorious First of June (1794), between the British and the French. The house is now Unsted Park School.

While you're there

Loseley House, just west of Godalming, is a splendid 16th-century house with lovely gardens. It was built in 1560 for Elizabeth I to stay in, and was also visited by James I. It has a superb library, and some wonderful panelling from Nonsuch Palace, one of Henry VIII's royal palaces. The Rose Garden boasts more than 1,000 bushes.

HYDON HEATH AND OCTAVIA HILL

DISTANCE/TIME	7.3 miles (11.7km) / 2hrs 45min
ASCENT/GRADIENT	1,106ft (337m) / ▲▲
PATHS	Woodland paths, farm tracks and some minor roads, 1 stile
LANDSCAPE	Wooded slopes and farmland of Wealden greensand ridge
SUGGESTED MAP	AA Walker's Map 23 Guildford, Farnham & The Downs
START/FINISH	Grid reference: SU979402
DOG FRIENDLINESS	Lead required through farmyards, near livestock and along roads
PARKING	National Trust Hydon's Ball car park on Salt Lane, near Hydestile
PUBLIC TOILETS	None on route

Imagine an organisation so big that its magazine has more readers than *The Times*, *Telegraph* and *Independent* put together. Imagine a landowner whose properties cover an area 30 per cent bigger than the county of Surrey. And imagine a club so popular that its membership outstrips the population of Birmingham, Leeds, Glasgow and Sheffield combined. That is the measure of the National Trust today. But this institution was founded by just three people – one a spinster who died several years before women had the right to vote.

At the top of Hydon's Ball, close to the start of this walk, you'll come to a massive granite bench in memory of that very lady. Octavia Hill was a social reformer in the same league as her contemporary, Florence Nightingale. She was born in Cambridgeshire in 1838, and after her father was bankrupted a few years later, Octavia and her mother moved to North London, where they began philanthropic work with the Christian Socialists. Octavia witnessed the appalling realities of life in the Dickensian backstreets, and these experiences inspired her great vocations: housing reform and countryside access.

Octavia's lifelong friend, John Ruskin, helped launch the first of her many housing improvement schemes and suggested ways of raising capital. Octavia Hill also wanted to protect areas of countryside where working people could enjoy their leisure time. She was appalled to see green fields disappearing under housing, and she joined the Commons Preservation Society to help safeguard 'open-air sitting rooms for the poor'. Later she became friends with the society's solicitor, Sir Robert Hunter. Towards the end of the century, Octavia and Sir Robert joined Canon Rawnsley in his fight for a Lake District beauty spot. This campaign brought together the founding triumvirate of the National Trust; they launched the idea in 1894, and the new organisation was incorporated in 1895. Soon after Octavia's death in 1912 the Trust bought 92 acres (37ha) at Hydon's Ball as her permanent memorial.

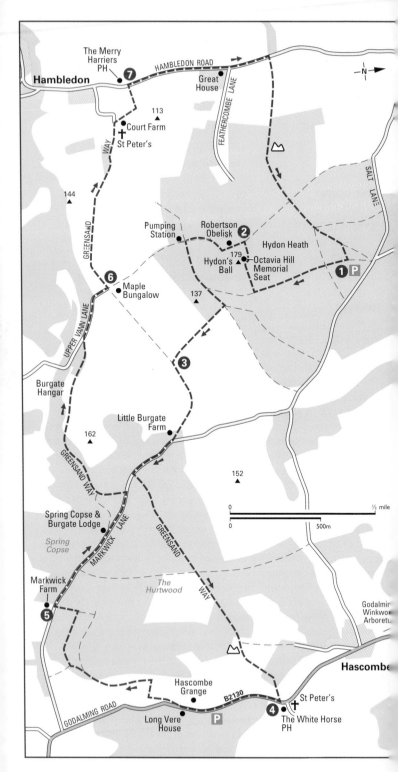

The Merry Harriers PH
HAMBLEDON ROAD
Hambledon
Great House
7
FEATHERCOMBE LANE
N
SALT LANE
113
Court Farm
St Peter's
GREENSAND WAY
144
Pumping Station
Robertson Obelisk
2
Hydon Heath
179
Hydon's Ball
Octavia Hill Memorial Seat
1 P
6
Maple Bungalow
137
UPPER VANN LANE
3
Burgate Hangar
Little Burgate Farm
162
152
GREENSAND WAY
Spring Copse & Burgate Lodge
Spring Copse
MARKWICK LANE
The Hurtwood
GREENSAND WAY
Godalming Winkworth Arboretum
Markwick Farm
5
0   ½ mile
0   500m
Hascombe
Hascombe Grange
B2130
4
St Peter's
GODALMING ROAD
Long Vere House
P
The White Horse PH

1. From the car park, with the road at your back, take the track beside a wide metal barrier uphill. At the crest of the hill, turn right and continue climbing, past a large green container, for 180yds (165m), to Octavia Hill's memorial seat. Continue ahead, and pass a low, green inspection cover for Hydon's Ball Reservoir on your right, and take the right fork downhill to a T-junction.

2. Turn left here. After 95yds (88m), you'll see the Robertson Obelisk on the right. Just beyond the memorial, turn right and descend to a forest crossroads close to a brick water-pumping station. Turn left; then, after 250yds (230m), fork right and continue to a junction 270yds (245m) further on. Turn right here, passing between two fields, then climb the old sunken way to a public bridleway marker post.

3. Turn left onto a wide sandy track and continue to Markwick Lane at Little Burgate Farm. Turn right; then, as the lane levels out, turn left to follow the Greensand Way signs. Follow this waymarked route as it climbs through the woods and then levels out through an area of managed woodland. Before the path starts to descend, turn right for a few paces and take the second path on the left. Drop steeply alongside a handrail, through a gate and alongside a field to another gate then straight ahead to The White Horse pub in Hascombe.

4. Turn right and follow the Godalming Road past Hascombe Grange. On the brow of the hill, opposite Long Vere House, cross the stile on your right. Follow the path and turn right towards the wood and follow the wood's perimeter to drop down left, with a post-and-wire fence, down the hill towards the red clay roofs of Markwick Farm.

5. Turn right on Markwick Lane and climb the hill to a bridleway signposting the Greensand Way. Turn left here, ignore the public footpath 170yds (155m) along on your left, and contour around the edge of Burgate Hangar until the bridleway drops left to join Upper Vann Lane. Follow the lane up the hill to reach Maple Bungalow, hidden in the trees.

6. Bear left at the fingerpost to follow the Greensand Way alongside a field on a level path to St Peter's Church, Hambledon. Just beyond the church, fork right and follow the public footpath to reach Hambledon Road opposite The Merry Harriers pub.

7. Turn right along Hambledon Road. Pass Feathercombe Lane, and, after 240yds (220m), turn right onto a bridleway between fields. The track enters the woods, and you climb steeply beside deer fencing, initially on both sides and then just on your right. Keep straight on at the end of the fencing, and after 95yds (88m), take the middle track ahead (purple arrow) at the three-way junction for the last 400yds (366m) to the car park.

Where to eat and drink

The Merry Harriers keeps real ales and has a great menu, a dining terrace and a large garden.

What to see

St Peter's Church at Hascombe rewards closer inspection. By 1863, it was so run down that Henry Woodyer was commissioned to design a new one, which is a remarkable example of Victorian architecture.

A CIRCUIT OF CHIDDINGFOLD

DISTANCE/TIME	3.2 miles (5.2km) / 1hr 45min
ASCENT/GRADIENT	230ft (70m) / ▲ ▲
PATHS	Broad and easy to follow through the village, bridleways near the river can get very muddy
LANDSCAPE	From Chiddingfold village across farmland and into woodland
SUGGESTED MAP	AA Walker's Map 23 Guildford, Farnham & The Downs
START/FINISH	Grid reference: SU959357
DOG FRIENDLINESS	Dogs on lead around Chiddingfold village and through farmland; let them off in the woods
PARKING	Coxcombe Lane car park, by playing fields in Chiddingfold
PUBLIC TOILETS	None on route

Chiddingfold is a very picturesque village with old buildings grouped around the village green. One of the oldest is The Crown Inn, which dates from the 13th century and may have been built by Cistercians as a resting place for itinerant monks. Folklore maintains that there was a tunnel between here and the church, but no trace of this has ever been found. It has certainly been used as an alehouse since 1353. It is believed that Queen Elizabeth I stayed at The Crown in 1591, while on her way to Cowdray Park in West Sussex. It is also said that King Edward VI, when his army was camped on the green in 1552, would probably have visited The Crown for refreshments.

Local industries

In the Middle Ages, Chiddingfold was highly regarded for the quality of the glass it produced. It was used in the windows of some of the finest buildings in the country, including St Stephen's Chapel in Westminster in 1351, and St George's Chapel in Windsor for Edward III. In the reign of Elizabeth I, there were 11 glass works around the village green. The villagers eventually petitioned to have them closed on the grounds that they were a nuisance – but, more probably, because of the foreigners who owned them. Replicas of Chiddingfold glass are still made, and one of the windows in St Mary's Church contains fragments of original Chiddingfold glass.

Another industry that has centred on Chiddingfold is the making of walking sticks. Back in the 1850s, they were made by three people in Chiddingfold. Many were made from chestnut and ash for walkers, and they had a wide variety of handles. Fashion canes, umbrella handles, ceremonial maces, and even hockey sticks and cudgels were also made here.

Despite its appearance as a sleepy village, Chiddingfold has attracted more than its fair share of musicians. During the 1970s, the Chiddingfold Club held concerts by the likes of Acker Bilk and Kenny Ball and, more recently Eric Clapton, Gary Brooker and the SAS Band. In the 1980s, the rock band Genesis bought a property in the village which they used as a rehearsal space, and The Stranglers, who also lived in the village, were even known at one time in their early days as The Chiddingfold Chokers.

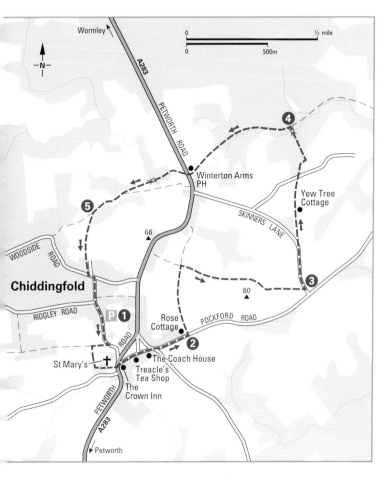

1. Turn left along Coxcombe Lane. Within 130yds (119m), as the lane bears to the left, turn right by the house, Beckhams, along a path that leads to St Mary's churchyard. On meeting another path, turn left into the churchyard. After visiting the church, continue along the path through the lychgate, and meet the A283 Petworth Road. Cross, with care, to walk past The Crown Inn and along the right side of the green. Continue to the top right-hand corner and The Coach House, and turn right, then left along Pockford Road. Pass Rose Cottage on the left, and take the next footpath left by the fingerpost.

2. Go through the gate and follow the path on the right side of a field. When the field widens, keep going straight ahead towards a line of trees. Remaining in the field, turn right and follow the path, keeping the hedge on your left.

At the second break in the hedge, just before passing under power lines, the path swerves left into the next field and continues in the same direction, with the hedge on your right-hand side and houses on your left, until it leads to a grassy path. At the next waymarker, turn left. The path winds through trees to Skinners Lane.

3. Turn left here. Walk along the road for 350yds (320m) and turn right onto a public footpath by the sign for Yew Tree Cottage. At the cottage, go ahead through the metal kissing gate and keep right through the field. At the far side, the path descends to another metal kissing gate, leading onto a metalled path. Turn right and, almost immediately left at the fingerpost down a public bridleway, with a wood on the left and paddocks to the right. The path bears left and descends into woodland and crosses a bridge to reach a cross-track.

4. Turn left by a waymarker along a public bridleway that meanders alongside the river (it can become muddy). It emerges close to the Winterton Arms on the A283 Petworth Road. Cross the road with care, go through a metal kissing gate and keep going ahead to take the public footpath opposite the pub. Pass through the next kissing gate onto a brick bridge and continue straight ahead, on the well-defined path. Soon you are confronted by two wooden plank bridges side by side.

5. Go over the left bridge and follow the path that crosses a field, heading towards the houses. At the far side it becomes a tree-lined walk, which reaches a metal gate and then a path by houses. At the end, turn left along Woodside Road. Take the next right down Coxcombe Lane, leading back to the car park.

Where to eat and drink
Halfway round the walk, the route passes the Winterton Arms, which serves good food. Alternatively, Chiddingfold village has the venerable Crown Inn, where you'll find top-quality food. There's also the attractive and comfortable Treacle's Tea Shop, offering snacks and beverages.

What to see
A surprise awaits in St Mary's churchyard. Hidden away in a fold of the ground is a brand new church meeting room. It was designed to have the lowest possible environmental impact, and is invisible from a distance. Its front has some beautiful glass doors, etched with birds and plants.

While you're there
South of Chiddingfold is Petworth House, a superb 17th-century mansion set in a huge deer park, managed by the National Trust. A splendid art collection is on display with pictures by Turner, Van Dyck, Reynolds and Blake along with sculpture, furniture, and carvings by Grinling Gibbons.

A CIRCUIT FROM WITLEY TO BROOK

DISTANCE/TIME	5.3 miles (8.5km) / 2hrs 30min
ASCENT/GRADIENT	558ft (170m) / ▲ ▲
PATHS	Woodland tracks and paths across farmland, some short sections on minor roads; 2 stiles
LANDSCAPE	Pretty landscape of small fields and wooded valleys
SUGGESTED MAP	AA Walker's Map 23 Guildford, Farnham & The Downs
START/FINISH	Grid reference: SU935399
DOG FRIENDLINESS	By law, dogs must be on lead through Furzefield Wood; strict control needed around livestock – bulls may be grazing here
PARKING	Mare Hill car park east of A286 on Roke Lane
PUBLIC TOILETS	None on route

As you head east along the edge of Witley Common on your way back towards Thursley, two grey stone lodges stand sentinel at the entrances to Witley Park. Nowadays, an exclusive business and conference centre lies beyond these gateways, but at the close of the 19th century the estate was put together by a very different kind of businessman. Whitaker Wright was a financier and self-made millionaire. In about 1890, Wright assembled a huge 9,000-acre (3,644ha) estate stretching from Thursley to the Devil's Punchbowl, and engaged leading architects and engineers to construct a vast mansion and lavish pleasure gardens, including the construction of dream-like follies.

Subterranean realm

One folly started with a hollow tree and a door. Beyond the door, a ramp spiralled down past subterranean rooms towards a flooded tunnel, 50ft (15m) below the ground. Climbing aboard the boat here, you felt your way through the tunnel until it brought you out onto a lake with an island. After rowing across to the island, a flight of stairs led down to a light, airy room directly below the island. More steps and another tunnel took you to the miniature iron and glass ballroom, submerged beneath the lake. Another tunnel led back into the warm sunshine, to ponder what all this must have cost...

It's said that Wright spent around £1.5m on Witley Park in the 1890s – perhaps as much as £200m by today's standards. By the turn of the century, his enterprises were collapsing. He was tried on charges of fraud at the Old Bailey, and sentenced to seven years' imprisonment. In an anteroom to the court, Whitaker Wright asked for a cigar and a glass of whisky – then swallowed a cyanide capsule to take his own life. Sadly, you cannot see any of Wright's follies. The house burned down and the present Witley Park Estate is not open to the public. Please keep to the rights of way described.

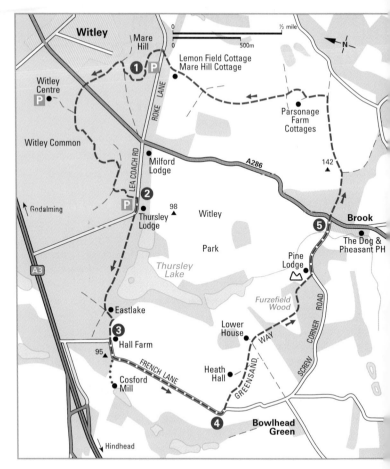

1. From the car park, and with your back to the road, take the path straight ahead. After 30yds (27m), turn left. After 100yds (91m), take the first fork right and descend on a winding, sandy path. After 150yds (137m), meet a T-junction and turn right, followed by a sharp left turn after a further 160yds (146m). Continue along this path to the A286. Go straight across and take the path immediately opposite onto Witley Common. After 20yds (18m), go ahead at the first cross-track, then right and, after a few paces, left at a larger crossroads. Continue on until the path meets a broad, sandy track coming from the left. Turn right at this point, fork left by a waymarker, and go straight on a cross-track before climbing uphill. At the purple marker, bear left up the hill and, meeting a cross-track, continue straight ahead to a National Trust car park.

2. Turn right along Lea Coach Road to Thursley Lodge. You'll get a glimpse of Witley Park down the private drive, but your route lies along the bridleway straight ahead, running parallel with a well-built stone wall on the left. The lane drops down to a junction; swing left past Eastlake and Lake Lodge, then bear right onto a woodland path.

3. Turn left on French Lane and continue ahead. At a signposted bridleway, you can take a short diversion to see a beautiful old watermill (now a private house) by forking right here and continuing downhill to the mill and its landscaped grounds. Retrace your steps back to French Lane and continue for 0.5 miles (0.8km), round a sharp left-hand bend.

4. Turn left onto the Greensand Way and continue through an avenue of trees, over a waymarked stile and around the left edge of a field. Halfway along, dodge left through a kissing gate and down some steps to the drive, cross the drive to Heath Hall and follow the waymarked Greensand Way through a gate, and then a kissing gate, and down an avenue of young trees. Pass through a gate and reach the entrance to Lower House, cross the drive and go through a kissing gate and continue straight down the slope and up the other side. Walk along a broad grassy track leading up to the edge of Furzefield Wood, turn left through the woods and down a short steep slope to Screw Corner Road by Pine Lodge.

5. Continue across the A286 and follow the Greensand Way until it turns off to the right, near the top of the hill. Keep straight on along the blue waymarked bridleway to Parsonage Farm Cottages and go left. After 22yds (20m), turn right through wooden posts onto a permitted footpath and follow the fence on your left to a gate at a three-way fingerpost. Go through the gate and head towards a pair of mature oak trees standing alone, on a public footpath running between two fences across the field, and to another gate on the far side. Cross the lane and go through another gate into the next field. Follow the path through the curving valley until two metal kissing gates and a wooden stile lead you past a pair of white cottages (Lemon Field Cottage and Mare Hill Cottage). Bear right up the drive to Roke Lane. Cross over and go down the footpath opposite. After 110yds (100m), turn left along a broad, sandy path. At the line of electricity wires turn left to return to the car park.

Where to eat and drink

A five-minute diversion at Brook brings you to the The Dog and Pheasant pub, where a wide range of snacks and bigger meals is available.

What to see

On Witley Common, look out for the National Trust's herd of Highland cattle. The brown woolly cattle are related to the Celtic longhorns, once used by Scottish crofters to provide meat, milk, clothing and motive power. Besides chomping through lower vegetation, so important in conserving the heathland, these beasts will happily push over 20ft (6m) birch trees to munch the leaves. Their long curved horns are every bit as fearsome as they look, so treat them with respect.

While you're there

Spend a little more time exploring the wonderful Witley and Milford Commons. Designated a Site of Special Scientific Interest, there is always something to see here, from fungi to purple heathers. There's a wealth of waymarked trails to follow, and it's also a great place for a picnic.

FROM COMPTON TO LITTLETON

DISTANCE/TIME	3.9 miles (6.2km) / 1hr 45min
ASCENT/GRADIENT	341ft (104m) / ▲
PATHS	Sandy tracks and field paths, can be muddy, 2 stiles
LANDSCAPE	Farmed and wooded countryside
SUGGESTED MAP	AA Walker's Map 23 Guildford, Farnham & The Downs
START/FINISH	Grid reference: SU963470
DOG FRIENDLINESS	Lead required through Coneycroft Farm and near livestock; not allowed in Watts Gallery
PARKING	Lay-by in Polsted Lane, close to junction with Withies Lane
PUBLIC TOILETS	Watts Gallery (for visitors only)

During the early 1880s, residents around London's Holland Park might have spotted one of their neighbours hauling an immense statue into his garden on a short length of railway track. The artist and sculptor George Frederic Watts began work on *Physical Energy*, possibly his greatest masterpiece, while living at his house in Melbury Road. Watts created this larger-than-life statue of a horse and rider purely for himself. He'd already created a plaster miniature and built the full-size version in a mixture of chalk, fibre and glue, supported on a wooden framework. You can see both models at the Watts Gallery in Compton – the finished bronze statue is now in Kensington Gardens, London.

Born in 1817, Watts was a sickly child and was educated at home. He studied briefly at the Royal Academy, but dropped out after only a few weeks. Despite this, he mastered the wide range of styles and techniques that you'll see at the gallery – social paintings, landscapes, allegorical works and sculptures. Described as the finest portrait painter of his generation, Watts gathered his best portraits into a 'Hall of Fame' that included artists, authors, scientists and people in public life, and gave this collection as his gift to the nation – a public record of the most influential Victorians around at a time when photography was still regarded as a passing fashion. As a result, most of these works are now held in the National Portrait Gallery.

In his personal life, too, Watts was a difficult person to classify. He married the charismatic actress Ellen Terry in 1864, when he was 47 and his bride was just 17; the consequences were predictable and the couple separated after only a year. It was over 20 years before Watts re-married, and in 1891 George and Mary Watts moved to Limnerslease, a new house at Compton designed for them by Ernest George. Here, Mary, also an artist, created the Mediterranean-style cemetery chapel, and the couple commissioned the Watts Gallery, the Arts and Crafts building that opened just before George's death in 1904.

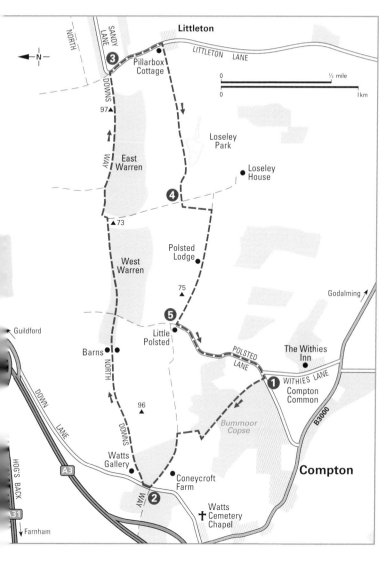

1. Take the signposted public footpath from the lay-by a few paces from the junction of Withies Lane and Polsted Lane. Head through Bummoor Copse, now much thinned on the left, then follow the enclosed path along the woodland edge until you reach a kissing gate at the end of a concrete farm road. Turn left along the road; then, just as you come to the large buildings at Coneycroft Farm, dodge up to your right and through a waymarked gate. Follow the narrow path out onto Down Lane.

2. Turn right for 27yds (25m) along the road. Just before the Watts Gallery, turn right again onto the signposted North Downs Way; this is easy walking, on a good track with sand under your feet. The track narrows as you pass farm buildings and begins the climb towards West Warren. At the signpost, stay with the North Downs Way across a bridleway and into the woods. As you

approach East Warren, the National Trail zig-zags left and right and joins a farm road. Follow it for another 700yds (640m) until the outskirts of Guildford come into view as the trail swings left at a waymark post.

3. Turn right; then, after 50yds (46m), keep ahead onto Littleton Lane. Follow it to the red postbox set into the garden wall of Pillarbox Cottage, and immediately turn right onto the signposted public footpath. The path leads you through a kissing gate and then across a couple of fields. There are picnic tables by the lake alongside the third field, and beyond a kissing gate enjoy great views of Loseley House on your left.

4. Cross a stile and walk over the track to Loseley House to reach a stile and a signpost. Follow the fenced path ahead as it bears round to the left. Continue, to emerge by the entrance to Loseley Park. Turn right and follow the track down a tree-lined avenue all the way through to Little Polsted at the top of Polsted Lane.

5. Turn left and follow the lane back to the junction at the start of the walk.

Where to eat and drink

For sandwiches, hot lunches, teas and cakes you can't beat the Tea Shop next to the Watts Gallery (it's open on the same days as the gallery). The Withies Inn is tucked away on Withies Lane. This 16th-century whitewashed free house serves bar snacks and a full restaurant menu, but is closed on Sunday evenings.

What to see

Take a short diversion along Down Lane to the Watts Cemetery Chapel in the graveyard at Compton. It was designed by George Watts' wife Mary, who was an artist in her own right. The little terracotta building is shaped like a Celtic cross. George and Mary's grave, with its moulded terracotta kerbstones, lies close to the cloister at the top of the hill.

While you're there

Visit the Watts Gallery to see an engaging exhibition of George Watts' work, from sketchbooks to towering statues. The museum is open Tuesday to Sunday, 11am to 5pm.

A DOUBLE LOOP
AT PIRBRIGHT

DISTANCE/TIME	4.8 miles (7.8km) / 2hrs 15min
ASCENT/GRADIENT	187ft (57m) / ▲
PATHS	Country roads, woodland tracks and paths, boggy in places, patchy waymarking, 2 stiles
LANDSCAPE	Wooded farmland conceals several massive houses on the edge of Pirbright army ranges
SUGGESTED MAP	OS Explorer 145 Guildford & Farnham
START/FINISH	Grid reference: SU946561
DOG FRIENDLINESS	Lead required along road and in woods south of Admiral's Walk
PARKING	On village green in Pirbright facing the cricket pitch
PUBLIC TOILETS	None on route

Whether or not Henry Morton Stanley actually delivered the famous line, 'Dr Livingstone, I presume?', when he tracked down the ailing missionary-explorer at Ujiji on Lake Tanganyika, the expression has passed into legend. So you can be forgiven for experiencing a profound sense of disbelief when your own expedition into deepest Surrey uncovers Stanley's grave in the corner of a village churchyard. You might expect to find it in Highgate Cemetery, perhaps – or, as Stanley himself had wished, next to the great Dr Livingstone in Westminster Abbey. But St Michael and All Angels, Pirbright? Well, sometimes fact can be stranger than fiction and, a few minutes into your walk, you'll come face to face with Stanley's powerfully simple memorial.

It's worth going back to the beginning of the story. In January 1841, Elisabeth Parry gave birth to an illegitimate child at Denbigh, in North Wales. The boy was baptised after his father, John Rowlands, who died just a couple of years later. Young John spent most of his childhood in the poverty-stricken surroundings of St Asaph's workhouse, until he ran away to sea and worked a passage to New Orleans in the US. There, he took the name of his adoptive father, an American merchant called Henry Morton Stanley. With his new identity, Stanley served in the Confederate Army during the American Civil War and went on to become a special correspondent for the *New York Herald*. At that time David Livingstone, who was in Africa searching for the source of the River Nile, had been out of touch for some five years. Most people believed him dead, but in 1869 Stanley accepted his editor's commission to find him.

It was March 1871 before Stanley led a company of around 2,000 men from Zanzibar into the uncharted African interior. Inevitably, there were problems – people deserted, disease was rife, and there were tribal conflicts along the way. Nevertheless, 700 miles (1,134km) and 236 days later, Stanley finally caught up with the ailing Livingstone and nursed him back to health. The two men went on to explore the northern end of Lake Tanganyika together before

Stanley returned to Europe in 1872. Stanley's subsequent expeditions opened up the heart of the African continent, and led to the foundation of the Belgian-dominated Congo Free State (later Zaire and now the Democratic Republic of Congo). His career in Africa ended with a three-year mission to rescue Mehmed Emin Pasha, a German explorer and provincial governor, who was pinned down by a native uprising.

In the closing years of the 19th century, Stanley returned to England, married, and moved to Furze Hill, near Pirbright. After five years as the Liberal Unionist MP for North Lambeth, he was knighted in 1899. He died in 1904.

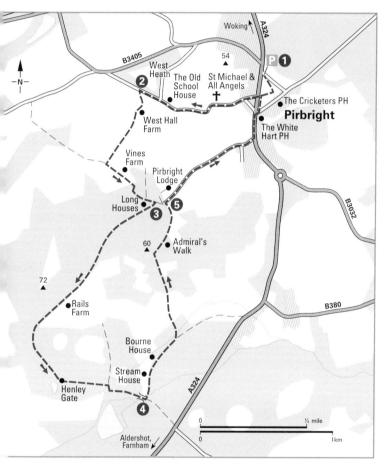

1. From the car park, face the cricket green and turn right. Follow the edge of the children's play area around to the right to meet the A324. Cross carefully and follow the lane towards the church, and turn into the churchyard at the little gate on your right. Just inside, you'll see Stanley's massive, roughly hewn memorial, bearing his African name 'Bula Matari' and the single word 'AFRICA'. His wife, Dorothy, and other members of the family lie in the same plot, edged with miniature standing stones and yew hedging. Don't miss the lovely interior of this beautifully kept Georgian church – and look, too, for Stanley's other

memorial, an inlaid brass plaque on the wall opposite the entrance. Leave the churchyard by the lychgate and turn right along the lane. Pass The Old School House and West Heath Road, and continue for 170yds (156m).

2. Turn left down the signposted bridleway towards West Hall Farm. Follow the track between the farmhouse and the barns, and join a green lane. Continue past Vines Farm to the edge of a small birchwood and turn left along the woodland bridleway. On reaching a T-junction, turn left under the power lines and then right; and, after a few paces, turn right again to pass a house hidden behind a high holly hedge. Just beyond the houses, turn left on a track, and continue to the junction of tracks near a postbox in the wall at Pirbright Lodge.

3. Double back hard right, and follow the broad track past Long Houses. At the meeting of seven tracks, go straight ahead along the waymarked footpath, and pass Rails Farm and several other cottages, where the track narrows briefly, before bearing left onto the Pirbright ranges perimeter track. As you approach the military barrier at Henley Gate, bear left onto a broad woodland footpath and follow it through to a T-junction. Turn right; then, 35yds (32m) further on, turn left onto a waymarked bridleway and continue until you cross a small concealed stream.

4. Turn left onto a signposted bridleway, pass Stream House, then follow the green lane just to the right of Bourne House. Continue for 330yds (302m) to a bridleway marker and turn left into the woods. Continue over a stile and then cross the plank bridge into a area of rough woodland. Climb over another stile and into a meadow before entering woodland again. Follow the path until it reaches a field with some stables and continue ahead on a wide path. At a gravel driveway, turn right, passing Admiral's Walk.

5. On reaching Pirbright Lodge, turn right and follow the lane out to the A324. Cross over, and turn left onto the roadside pavement that leads you back to the green where your walk began.

Where to eat and drink

Facing onto Pirbright Common is The White Hart, dating from 1650 and said to be haunted. It has flagstone floors, beamed ceilings and roaring fires in winter, and serves good food and real ales. The Cricketers, also on the village green, serves a range of snacks and bar meals.

What to see

In the woods between Stream House and Admiral's Walk, you'll walk between clumps of rhododendron bushes. Introduced from the Himalayas to provide cover for pheasants on sporting estates, these huge shrubs thrive on acid soils.

While you're there

Take a tour of the Hog's Back Brewery and see the brewers at work. Tour times are flexible, but should be booked in advance – visit www.hogsback. co.uk for details. The brewery is based at Manor Farm, Tongham, just off the Hog's Back ridge on the outskirts of Farnham, and the brewery shop is open seven days a week.

PUTTENHAM COMMON AND PUTTENHAM

DISTANCE/TIME	4 miles (6.4km) / 1hr 45min
ASCENT/GRADIENT	423ft (129m) / ▲ ▲
PATHS	Woodland tracks and field-edge paths, 4 stiles
LANDSCAPE	Wooded heath and farmland
SUGGESTED MAP	AA Walker's Map 23 Guildford, Farnham & The Downs
START/FINISH	Grid reference: SU920461
DOG FRIENDLINESS	Can run free on Puttenham Common, lead required in village and over farmland
PARKING	Puttenham Common top car park, on Suffield Lane
PUBLIC TOILETS	None on route

The railway line no longer runs to Hayfield, high in the Derbyshire Peak District. With it have passed many of the 400 people who gathered at the little station for the mass trespass on Kinder Scout in 1932. The 1930s saw an explosion of interest in walking, and the Kinder Scout trespass was a landmark along the way to the legislation which underpins the modern family of National Trails. First was the Pennine Way, opened in 1965, but other routes were soon to follow. In September 1978, the North Downs Way was officially opened between Farnham and Dover, and you'll follow a section of it on your way through Puttenham today. In many places the route follows the old Pilgrims' Way that runs from Winchester, through Farnham and Guildford to Canterbury.

Tales from the trail

This National Trail has a loop that allows modern-day pilgrims to visit Canterbury on their way to or from Dover, but you don't need to walk all the way to Becket's cathedral to enjoy a few stories of the road. About 400yds (366m) before you reach the North Downs Way, near the entrance to a Woodland Trust property on your right, you'll pass a bridleway that was part of the old carriage drive to Hampton Park. Legend has it that when playwright Richard Brinsley Sheridan was visiting his friend Edward Long at Hampton in the early 19th century, his coach turned over at this spot. Long subsequently planted seven trees to mark the route – one for each of his daughters.

General James Oglethorpe (1699–1785), a philanthropist and social reformer who founded the American state of Georgia, where he hoped to settle some of Britain's poorest residents, bought the Puttenham Estate in 1744. MP for Haslemere and a leading humanitarian, he mingled with many of the great people of the age, including John Wesley, Thomas Paine and Samuel Johnson, and was instrumental in founding a number of British hospitals, university colleges and the British Museum. The General's Pond, near Puttenham middle car park, is named after him. However, he actually lived in Godalming, and he sold the estate in 1761. The new owner demolished the little manor house and replaced it with the Palladian mansion that you'll see from the footpath off Suffield Lane at Point 4 on your walk, just after leaving the North Downs Way. Although Oglethorpe named it The Priory (now Puttenham Priory), the building never had any religious connections.

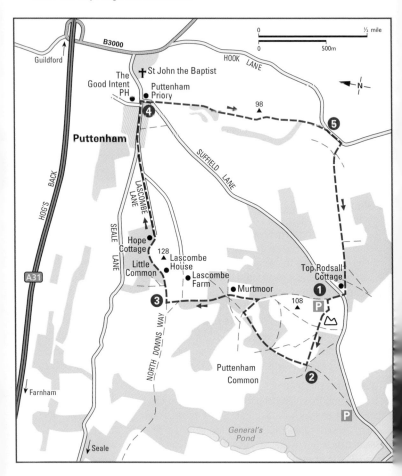

1. Facing the view from the car park, take the right-hand path, beside a litter bin, to drop down into the trees on a series of wide steps. At the bottom, take the first right and then left at the cross-tracks a few paces further on. Dodge in and out of the trees with a wide open area to your right.

2. At a five-way junction, just within the trees, turn right up a rough avenue of oak trees. At the next cross-tracks continue ahead, and the sandy track becomes grassy. At the next junction, fork left down an overgrown path. The path descends, and then turns left; and, at a bridleway marker, turn right up a sunken path to emerge opposite a four-way fingerpost beneath telephone lines. Turn left and at the first telegraph pole turn right. Pass a wooden barrier and, on reaching a gravel driveway, turn left. Pass two houses and rise up a

slope beneath telephone lines, and follow them ahead. When the lines turn right, continue ahead passing Lascombe House on the right. Go onto the common, straight ahead to meet the North Downs Way.

3. Turn sharp right here and follow the North Downs Way as it winds over Little Common and continues through Puttenham.

4. Turn right opposite The Good Intent pub into Suffield Lane. As the lane swings to the right, cross the stile by the footpath signposted 'The Fox Way' on your left, and follow the left-hand edge of a field to the trees on the far side. Just before a metal gate (private property), dodge right to take the waymarked route beside a second stile. Continue along the edge of woodland, over a fallen tree, with a post-and-wire fence on your left-hand side, until a stile and kissing gate lead into an open field. Following the yellow waymark post, walk straight across the field, heading for the shortest oak tree, on the far right of a line of trees, and then through another kissing gate. Now keep ahead, following the waymarked path, and bear right down a short, sharp slope and bend right beneath power lines to a kissing gate leading out onto Hook Lane.

5. Turn right and follow the road to the left-hand bend. Turn right again, over the stile by a public footpath sign. Walk alongside a fence, which can be overgrown, and then onto a wide grassy track; at a cross-tracks keep ahead. Continue to a small wood, go through a broken kissing gate onto an old sunken lane, and keep ahead for 150yds (137m) to a small waymark post. Continue straight on, following a small public footpath sign, to a T-junction with a bridleway. Turn left and in 15yds (14m) turn right up some steps on a public footpath. Climb steeply here, for the short way back to Suffield Lane and the entrance to the car park at the walk's start.

Where to eat and drink
In Puttenham, The Good Intent pub on The Street opposite Point 4 serves real ales and bar meals.

What to see
Visit the Church of St John the Baptist in Puttenham. As you enter the churchyard you'll see an old well on the left. It was filled in and forgotten until 1972, when it dramatically reappeared during morning service on Palm Sunday, as the first of a line of newly planted yew trees suddenly disappeared down the well.

While you're there
Manor Farm Craft Centre is in Seale village, just along from Puttenham. You can visit the craftspeople and watch demonstrations. There's a tea room, too. Closed Mondays, except bank holidays.

HINDHEAD AND THE DEVIL'S PUNCH BOWL

DISTANCE/TIME	3.5 miles (5.7km) / 2hrs 15min
ASCENT/GRADIENT	791ft (241m) / ▲ ▲ ▲
PATHS	Mostly broad, unmade woodland tracks
LANDSCAPE	Plunging, dramatic woods and heathland
SUGGESTED MAP	OS Explorer 145 Guildford & Farnham
START/FINISH	Grid reference: SU890357
DOG FRIENDLINESS	Take special care at A3 crossings; strict control around grazing livestock
PARKING	National Trust car park on A3, just east of Hindhead (free to NT members)
PUBLIC TOILETS	At car park

Today, Hindhead Common and the Devil's Punch Bowl are renowned beauty spots, lovingly cared for by the National Trust. Yet just three centuries ago this desolate area was dreaded by travellers on the Portsmouth road. Daniel Defoe thought it barren and sterile, 'horrid and frightful to look on', and even after the road was turnpiked and improved in 1749, travellers were not entirely safe.

Murder on the road

One Sunday in September 1786, an unknown sailor with money in his pocket was making his way towards Portsmouth when he fell into the company of three other travellers: Michael Casey, Edward Lonegon and James Marshall. One of these three was apparently a former shipmate, and the four of them stopped at The Red Lion in Thursley for food and drink. The trio, it seems, were penniless, so their new-found friend paid the bill before they all set off over the Devil's Punch Bowl towards Portsmouth. We shall never know whether the brutal murder on the summit east of Hindhead was anything more than simple robbery. But, whatever the motive, Casey, Lonegon and Marshall set about their companion, stabbing him repeatedly before stripping his body, rolling it down the hill into the Punch Bowl, and scurrying off towards Liphook. The spot is still marked by a memorial stone erected 'in detestation of a barbarous murder committed here on an unknown sailor' – look out for it on the left of the old road on the diversion up to Gibbet Hill, just after the start of this walk.

This may have been a lonely, windswept heath, but the murder didn't go unobserved. Several people had seen the four men leave the inn at Thursley, and by chance two of them happened to be taking the self-same road. They saw the attack on the sailor, found his mutilated body and hurried back to Thursley to raise the alarm. It wasn't long before Casey, Lonegon and Marshall were overtaken and arrested in The Sun Inn at Rake, near Petersfield. The three murderers were held in Guildford jail until their trial at Kingston in April 1787, when they pleaded guilty to 'wilful murder and robbing'. Their total haul was valued at £1 7s 6d – about £130 in today's money. The three men were hanged just two days later. Their bodies were coated in tar, and hung in chains from a great iron wheel mounted on a tall wooden post. The execution spot is still known as Gibbet Hill, and a Celtic cross now stands on the summit.

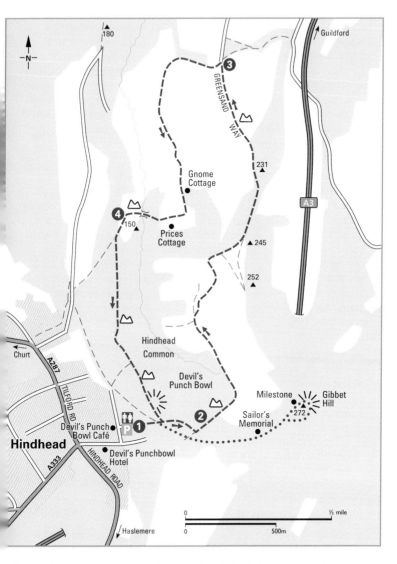

1. Head from the car park towards Devil's Punch Bowl along the track between the café and the information board. Continue ahead to reach the viewing platform, marked by a bronze relief map of the Devil's Punch Bowl, overlooking a spectacular view. Descend the few steps and then turn right along the path. After 100yds (91m), meet a fork in the paths with a gate on the left-hand path. (At this point you can take a simple, short there-and-back (1.miles/1.8km) route to Gibbet Hill by following the right-hand path and NT blue-and-pink trail

markers: the route continues ahead, crosses over the line of the old road at an information board, and then shortly turns left on a tarmac path that leads past the Sailor's Memorial and then, 60yds (55m) later, turns right to Gibbet Hill. Afterwards, turn left to the Celtic cross and down a short narrow path to the tarmac path, turn left and retrace your steps to the junction of paths.)

2. Now take the left fork to pass through a wooden kissing gate. Continue past two seats close together; and, in a further 85yds (73m), reach steep steps on the left. Descend these 102 steps and follow the narrow path as it drops into the valley. At the bottom meet a broad path coming from the right and turn left. At the next cross-path, near a Roam 639 waymarker, turn right and walk uphill to a wooden kissing gate. Go through the gate, turn left and then right onto tarmac track to a staggered junction of four tracks, where the Greensand Way joins from the right. Take the track on the left, the continuation of the Greensand Way, also marked 'Unsuitable for motor vehicles'. Continue until meeting another four-way cross-tracks.

3. Turn left off the Greensand Way, signed 'Café 1.75 miles', and bear gently right just beyond a waymark post 60yds (55m) further on. The unsurfaced track is easy to follow as it winds down into the valley, ignoring paths from the left and right. Continue straight ahead as another track leads in from the right opposite a bench seat, with open views to the woodland across the valley. Keep straight on through the gate beside the cattle grid, and pass Gnome Cottage nestled in the trees to your left, then climb on a metalled track to a seat at a T-junction. Turn right, signed to 'Café 1 mile'. When the main track bears left towards Prices Cottage, continue ahead on narrower path, down some steps to a small wooden footbridge. Cross the brook here, and make the short, sharp climb up the sunken lane opposite.

4. Turn left at the top through a kissing gate onto a delightful wooded track, waymarked 'Highcombe Hike'. Just around a left-hand bend, keep to the lower, left-hand fork, again waymarked 'Highcombe Hike'. Pass through a kissing gate; this is the start of a 0.5-mile (800m) steady but unremitting ascent to the summit, where you meet the gate you passed through earlier. Turn right and then bear left back to the car park.

Where to eat and drink

The Devil's Punch Bowl Café serves hot and cold food and has tables inside and out. There is also a useful collection of books, maps and information. Alternatively, try the Devil's Punchbowl Hotel for meals.

What to see

A Celtic cross stands near the old Ordnance Survey triangulation pillar at the top of Gibbet Hill, and a plate points out views to places as far afield as Winchester (26 miles/42km), Portsmouth (27 miles/43km), East Grinstead (30 miles/48km) and London (38 miles/61km).

While you're there

Once described as a 'mini British Museum', Haslemere's Educational Museum covers everything from botany and zoology to archaeology and European folk art. Open Tuesday to Saturday, 10am to 5pm.

HANKLEY COMMON TO THURSLEY

DISTANCE/TIME	3 miles (4.9km) / 1hr 45min
ASCENT/GRADIENT	315ft (96m) / ▲ ▲
PATHS	Sandy paths across heathland, some steeper paths in woodland
LANDSCAPE	Mostly heathland, with some pretty paths and lanes around the village of Thursley
SUGGESTED MAP	AA Walker's Map 23 Guildford, Farnham & The Downs
START/FINISH	Grid reference: SU891411
DOG FRIENDLINESS	Dogs can run free across Hankley Common, but leads required on Thursley National Nature Reserve
PARKING	Hankley Common car park on Thursley Lane
PUBLIC TOILETS	None on route; nearest at Frensham Great Pond Visitor Centre

Thursley is a very pretty village that forms the centre point of this walk. It has all the elements of a classic English village – a squat, largely Anglo-Saxon church with a sundial on the bell tower instead of a clock, many attractive old houses, a pub, a cricket ground and cricket teams. In the past this was largely an agricultural area, but in the 17th century it became a centre for iron smelting when it produced cannon and shot for the Royal Navy, and in the early 19th century it had a thriving silk industry.

The architect Edwin Lutyens grew up in the village, and Monica Edwards, the children's writer best known for her Romney Marsh and Punchbowl Farm series of children's novels, lived at Punch Bowl Farm for a time. Sir Malcolm Arnold, who composed many film scores, including the one for *The Bridge on the River Kwai* (1957) for which he won an Academy Award, also lived in the village in the 1960s.

Thursley Common

Today it is a peaceful spot, surrounded by lovely countryside that is rich in wildlife. Thursley is lucky enough to have a National Nature Reserve on its doorstep, and this walk goes through part of it. The reserve is one of the largest surviving areas of Surrey heath and supports a variety of rare wildlife. Although this walk visits only the heathland areas, other parts are much damper, with bog pools and sphagnum lawns. This is one of the best sites in Britain for dragonflies, with 26 species having been recorded. There are also sundews, marsh orchids and bog asphodel. Some rare birds nest in the area, including the Dartford warbler, and there is a good chance you will see the eye-catchingly beautiful silver-studded blue butterfly on your walk.

The Nature Reserve is part of Thursley Common, which suffered terrible fires in 2006. They lasted for five days and damaged around 60 per cent of the area. More than 120 firefighters were involved and, at first, it was feared that the losses were irreversible. The heathland is recovering, but the event had a major impact on the community, and references to it can be found in Thursley's church on a splendid pair of modern glass vestry doors. Walking through Thursley Common today shows how resilient nature can be.

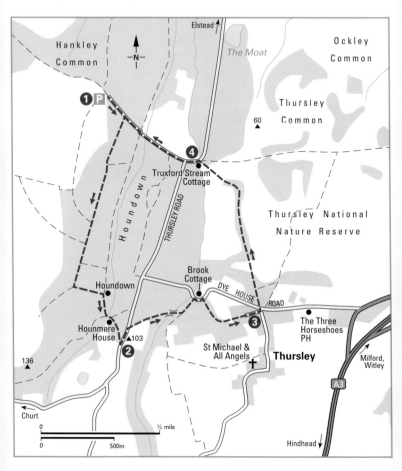

1. From the entrance to the car park, turn right along a tarmac road for about 120yds (110m), turn right by telegraph pole 11, passing a metal barrier, and walk along a straight, sandy track, lined with pine trees, and carry straight on into open heathland, with the power lines to your right. Continue walking past pylons to reach pylon 23; and, immediately afterwards, turn left down a track that descends and curves left. At a T-junction, turn right down a sandy path beneath power cables and continue uphill near a house called Houndown, parallel to another path by some houses. As the path forks under power cables, take the left fork along a path, which descends and meets another track coming in from the right. Pass a barrier to meet a tarmac track and turn right. Turn right again near the entrance to Hounmere House to follow a public bridleway. Ascend to meet Thursley Road.

2. Turn left and, in about 100yds (91m), turn right along a public footpath that descends and crosses a wooden bridge. Pass through at a wooden gate to enter a pretty grassy area with a small stream. Keep to the left side and bear right to cross a wooden bridge. Continue with the fence on the left, cross a wooden boardwalk and head for a gate. Turn left at the fingerpost to follow a public footpath along a tarmac track. On meeting a road at Brook Cottage, turn right and follow it as it ascends and curves left. At a fingerpost and a 30mph sign, turn right along a public footpath, walking uphill and then fork right through woods. Emerge onto a tarmac drive by some houses and continue ahead to reach a triangular green.

3. Turn left to reach the main road and cross to a fingerpost opposite, then take the public bridleway, turning left after 22yds (20m). At a cross-track, go straight ahead, and bear left at the next cross-track onto a broad, sandy track, following the public bridleway. Continue on the main track, which curves right at the next waymarker. On meeting a path coming in from the right, turn left and immediately bear left at the next fork, keeping the field on the left. Ignore side tracks as the path widens.

4. Meet Thursley Road, just beyond Truxford Stream Cottage, and turn left. Then, as the road bears left, turn right along a public bridleway, signed to October Farm, to return to the car park.

Where to eat and drink
A short stroll along the main street of Thursley, turning right at Point 3, will bring you to The Three Horseshoes, a welcoming and traditional village pub with a strong local feel to it. The food is splendid, with plenty of local produce, and there's a lovely patio and garden, friendly staff and roaring fires in winter. Dogs and children are welcome, too.

What to see
The village church is worth a detour off the route at Point 3 in Thursley. Turn right along The Street and you will soon reach the Church of St Michael and All Angels. It is a very old building with some 11th-century windows. It also has a brand-new set of glass vestry doors, which are wonderful to study. They include engravings of trees, birds and butterflies, reflecting the local landscape, and include references to the terrible fires on the common in 2006.

While you're there
The Witley Centre, 4 miles (6.4km) from Thursley, is a good place to learn about the wildlife and habitats of the area. Run by the National Trust, it has some excellent displays. Witley Common lies to the east of Thursley Common, and they share some similar features.

47

MYTCHETT TO FRIMLEY

DISTANCE/TIME	2.1 miles (3.3km) / 1hr
ASCENT/GRADIENT	66ft (20m) / Negligible
PATHS	Canal towpath and level tracks through woodland
LANDSCAPE	Canalside views and light woodland
SUGGESTED MAP	OS Explorer 145 Guildford & Farnham
START/FINISH	Grid reference: SU893549
DOG FRIENDLINESS	Enjoyable walking for dogs
PARKING	Basingstoke Canal Centre
PUBLIC TOILETS	Basingstoke Canal Centre and Frimley Lodge Park

The Basingstoke Canal today is a thriving stretch of waterway, with canal boat trips and traditional narrow boats to be found chugging along much of its length. It was not always so. Back in 1966 a group of enthusiasts got together to try to reopen the derelict canal. Eleven years later work started to restore a flight of locks at Deepcut, just north of this walk. There followed a further 14 years of work before the canal was formally reopened in 1991, and restoration work continues. The use of the canal has greatly increased, and the Canal Centre at the start of this walk shows graphically what has been achieved.

The canal originally ran from Basingstoke to Weybridge, where it joined the River Thames. The connection with the Thames has been restored and the canal is now open again as far as Greywell, 5 miles (8km) from its original destination. The Greywell Tunnel is blocked and has been taken over by bats – indeed, it is a Site of Special Scientific Interest and has more roosting bats, of several different species, than anywhere else in Britain. Nowadays the only way to complete the route to Basingstoke is along the Canal Heritage Footpath.

The canal story

The canal was constructed between 1789 and 1794, and the original business plan had been to stimulate the development of agriculture in Hampshire. One of the main commodities carried in the early days was timber from Basingstoke. Fir trees were planted along stretches of the canal to exploit this trade. Other items carried on the barges included chalk, milk and flour. Coal and groceries came down the canal from London. By 1822, however, the cost of transporting goods by road was much the same as it was by barge, and it was quicker. The building of the railway from London to Southampton also took business away, but there was a temporary reprieve when the army camp was built at Aldershot. Nevertheless, by 1866 the company was in liquidation.

Various initiatives tried to keep the canal going. It was used during World War I to move munitions, and during World War II as a line of defence (a number of concrete pill boxes can be found along its length). However, it was effectively derelict by the mid-1960s, when the local enthusiasts took up the challenge to restore it. Before starting the walk, pop into the Canal Centre. There is a small museum on the history of the Basingstoke Canal, a shop, a children's play area and a café. There are also boats to hire.

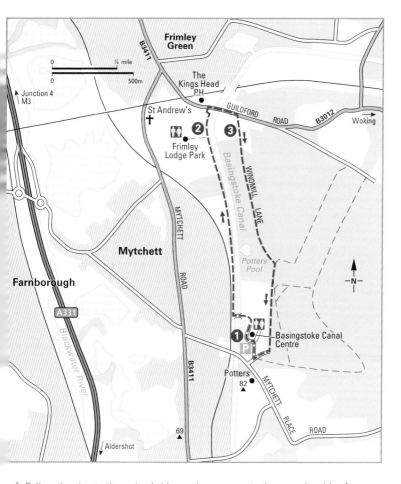

1. Follow the sign to the swing bridge and cross over to the opposite side of the canal. Turn right and follow the canal towpath towards Frimley Lodge Park. After 390yds (356m), you will see Potter's Pool on the right. This is rich in wildlife, particularly dragonflies. Beyond Potter's Pool it is another 0.5 miles (880m) to reach Frimley Lodge Park.

2. This is a large area devoted to a variety of activities, and the small café is a good pit stop. Continuing past Frimley Lodge Park, it is only 120yds (110m) to the Guildford Road bridge. Just before the bridge the path turns left and then right to reach the road. Cross over the road and turn right to walk over the bridge. Once over the bridge, cross back over the road to the pavement on the right-hand side. After 90yds (82m), turn right, just before a red pillar box, down Windmill Lane, a public bridleway.

3. The gravel bridleway narrows, and, at the end, go through a metal gate into woodland. Continue straight ahead, over a crossroads of tracks and under telephone lines. After 960yds (877m), reach a T-junction and turn right. Continue straight on to reach the boundary of an MOD area with its warning signs. Go straight on here, with a wire fence on your right and a field behind it. Follow the fence, passing a small housing development on the right and follow the track right. On reaching a junction with a track coming from the left, turn right and pass to the side of a metal barrier. Continue to Mytchett Place Road, with Potters (restaurant/bar) in front. Turn right to meet the entrance road to the Basingstoke Canal Centre and return to the car park.

Where to eat and drink
The café at the Basingstoke Canal Centre provides a good range of food and drink that you can enjoy indoors or out, and is open daily (Easter to September) or Monday to Friday (October to March). It is also close to the children's play area, which is handy for families. Snacks are also available from the small café at Frimley Lodge Park.

What to see
While you are at the Basingstoke Canal Centre have a look at the museum. There is an interactive model of a lock to show how it works, and a replica of a canal boat cabin to interest those who have never been in one.

While you're there
The story of flight in Britain began in Farnborough, and the FAST Museum there has an interesting exhibition of the work of the pioneers of flight in this country, as well as a full-size replica of the first aeroplane to take to the air in this country. You can also try to fly it using the simulator. Admission is free but donations are welcome.

WAVERLEY AND TILFORD

DISTANCE/TIME	3.5 miles (5.7km) / 1hr 30min
ASCENT/GRADIENT	253ft (77m) / ▲
PATHS	Sandy and easy to follow, two sections on minor roads
LANDSCAPE	Gently rolling, well-wooded countryside
SUGGESTED MAP	AA Walker's Map 23 Guildford, Farnham & The Downs
START/FINISH	Grid reference: SU870455
DOG FRIENDLINESS	Generally good, but lead essential along roads
PARKING	Waverley Lane between Farnham and Elstead
PUBLIC TOILETS	None on route

The glory of this walk lies right at the start, just a stone's throw across the fields from the car park. For over 400 years Waverley Abbey stood in this peaceful loop of the northern River Wey, and from here its abbots wielded huge religious and political influence. It all began in 1128 when William Gifford, Bishop of Winchester, founded Waverley on 60 acres (24ha) of farmland. This was the first Cistercian abbey in England, and the original community of 12 monks came with Abbot John from L'Aumône in France. They lived an austere life of manual labour and unceasing prayer.

Construction started at once, although it was another 150 years before the abbey church was finally completed. Meanwhile, the Cistercians expanded rapidly throughout Britain, and by 1132 there were great abbeys at Tintern, Fountains and Rievaulx. Waverley itself was the springboard for 13 new monasteries – in each case an abbot and 12 monks, representing Christ and his 12 disciples, went forward as the nucleus of the new community.

At Waverley, as elsewhere, the monks had an impact on the local economy as they converted the surrounding forests into grazing and arable fields. They began Surrey's wool industry, and extended their hospitality from the humblest to the greatest. The lavish scale of monastic entertaining seems decadent, but these were exceptions to the harsh, everyday routine. Monks rose at 2am for Matins, spending their time in meditation, study and manual work before retiring as early as 5.30pm in winter. The day was punctuated by eight services, and by the midday meal. You'll see the remains of the refectory with its 13th-century vaulting during your visit. Look, too, for the walls of the Chapter House, where the Abbot presided over the daily business meeting.

Of the church, only the ground plan and some parts of the chancel walls remain to give you an idea of the scale of the building. The monastic community continued until it was suppressed by Henry VIII in 1536. The estate changed hands many times. Inevitably, over the years the buildings were quarried for stone, and many wagon loads found their way into the construction of nearby Loseley House.

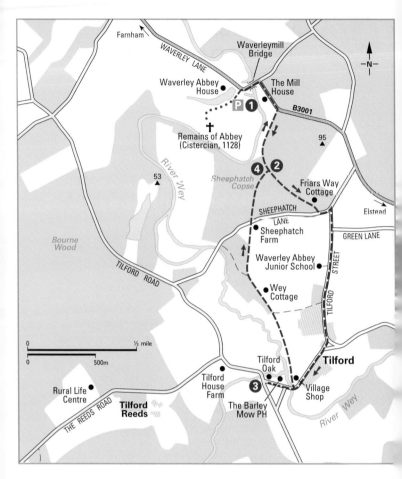

1. Turn right out of the car park, taking care to check for traffic, and follow Waverley Lane (B3001) as it crosses over Waverleymill Bridge. Continue for 200yds (182m) until the road bears to the left, before turning right onto the public byway.

2. Keep straight ahead and follow the path through a gate and past Friars Way Cottage, then through another gate to reach Sheephatch Lane. Turn left briefly, then right at the junction with Tilford Street; there's no pavement for the first 400yds (366m), so go carefully. Now follow the road past the school, village shop, over the River Wey bridge and on to Tilford village green, where you'll find the Tilford Oak and The Barley Mow pub.

3. To continue, retrace your steps across the river. Almost at once, turn left at the public bridleway sign, passing a pair of World War II pillboxes. The path climbs gently for 500yds (457m) and brings you to a tarmac lane. Turn left at a bridleway sign, pass some houses and continue up the narrow, sandy track straight ahead. At the top of the short slope, fork right at the public byway waymark for the 400yds (366m) climb to Sheephatch Farm. Cross Sheephatch Lane, where a public byway sign points your way up the gravelled track

opposite. The track leads you confidently through Sheephatch Copse, and soon you'll be dropping down on an ancient sunken way to rejoin your outward track at a public byway signpost.

4. Turn left here for the easy walk back to Waverley Lane (B3001). Watch out for the traffic as you turn left, then retrace your outward route over Waverleymill Bridge and back to the car park.

Extending the walk You can extend this walk by 0.6 miles (0.9km) by visiting Waverley Abbey. From the car park, go through the wooden kissing gate and follow the level gravel path, with the pond and Waverley Abbey House to your right. At the gate, go through a metal turnstile and turn right, then continue through the wooden gate to explore the abbey ruins. Afterwards, retrace your steps to the car park.

Where to eat and drink

Halfway round your walk, relax in The Barley Mow pub with its spacious garden, delightfully situated overlooking Tilford's village green. Cricket is played here, and you'll find a good choice of bar snacks and restaurant meals and, in the summer, a BBQ and summer 'outdoor' bar in operation. Teas, coffees and sandwiches can be purchased in the village shop.

What to see

Beside the green at Tilford, the Tilford Oak is said to be at least 800 years old. William Cobbett thought it the finest tree that he ever saw in his life, but now its branches have been lopped and the trunk is patched with iron sheets. When it was measured in July 1907, its circumference was 24ft 9in (7.5m); in 1934, it was exactly 1ft (30cm) more. Opposite this mighty specimen stands a mere sapling, planted in 1902 to commemorate the coronation of Edward VII. At the other end of the green, another tree dates from Queen Victoria's Jubilee in 1897. Keep your eyes peeled for a glimpse of a green woodpecker. It's the largest British woodpecker, and you won't mistake this conspicuous bright green bird with its crimson cap and yellow rump. Although it excavates its own nesting hole in a tree, the green woodpecker also spends a lot of time on the ground, probing for insects with its long pointed beak.

While you're there

Spread out over 10 acres (3.7ha) of field and woodland, Tilford's Rural Life Centre presents a vivid recreation of local country life over the last 150 years. You'll see realistic settings including everything from agriculture and hop growing to the rural post office and wheelwright's workshop. There's also a shop, café, picnic area and children's playground, and you can ride the Old Kiln Light Railway on Sundays and bank holidays. Open Wednesday to Sunday (and bank holidays), March to October; and Wednesday and Sunday only, November to February.

FRENSHAM AND SPREAKLEY

DISTANCE/TIME	4.2 miles (6.8km) / 2hrs
ASCENT/GRADIENT	417ft (127m) / ▲ ▲
PATHS	Farmland, some woodland and sandy paths on heathland, and a muddy path beside the river, 6 stiles
LANDSCAPE	From Frensham Pond up to a ridge with splendid views
SUGGESTED MAP	AA Walker's Map 23 Guildford, Farnham & The Downs
START/FINISH	Grid reference: SU845405
DOG FRIENDLINESS	Generally off lead, but not on farmland
PARKING	Frensham Pond Visitor Centre (pay and display at the weekend)
PUBLIC TOILETS	Frensham Pond Visitor Centre

Frensham Great Pond is well known for its variety of wildlife, particularly birds. Some years ago, Dartford warblers started nesting on the nearby common, and stonechats are a regular sighting. In most years an osprey will visit the area, and other unusual birds are regularly spotted. The pond was first dug in around 1200 as a fish pond for the Bishop of Winchester, and stocked with bream, pike and carp. While it was managed as a fish farm it was drained every five years to collect the fish. Most recently, it was drained during World War II to prevent it being used as a landmark by enemy aircraft. Some years before that it was the location for testing Britain's first seaplane.

King's Ridge

At the start of the walk and looking to the east, a ridge can be seen running parallel with the road. This is known as the King's Ridge because King Edward VII reviewed the troops from here. It is a very ancient site, however, and there are Bronze Age burial mounds on the top. As you leave the pond you pass the pond outfall, which was a mill in the time of Edward VI (1537–1553).

The walk weaves round to visit the village of Frensham. There has been a settlement in this area since Mesolithic times. It was a popular hunting area for the kings of England in the Middle Ages, and the church dates from 1239, although there was an earlier building on the site. A curiosity to be found in the church is a large cauldron, said to have belonged to a local witch, Mother Ludlum. The legend goes that when the cauldron was stolen by the Devil, Mother Ludlum gave chase. The story goes that the Devil eventually dropped the cauldron, and Mother Ludlum then moved it to Frensham Church for safe keeping. A more prosaic explanation is that the pot is typical of those used in the Middle Ages for preparing food for weddings and other village events. In any event, the church at Frensham is very beautiful and well worth exploring.

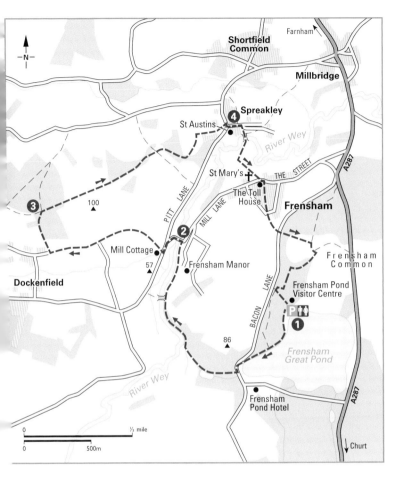

1. From the car park, face Frensham Great Pond and take the sandy path in the bottom right corner, close to the pond. Keep left, following the fence. Walk alongside the pond until you reach Bacon Lane. Turn left and continue until you meet some metal railings on the right. Turn right along a public bridleway that follows the overflow to the pond and leads to the north branch of the River Wey. At a fork, keep to the higher right-hand path. Pass a bridge on the left, and follow the path to a gravel drive and The Mill House on the left.

2. Continue to Mill Lane and turn left, passing over a bridge. Walk down Mill Lane to Pitt Lane and turn left. Before reaching Mill Cottage, turn right up a public bridleway and follow this round between fields towards houses. Just before reaching them, turn right and cross a stile onto a public footpath. This leads up a field towards a small wood and a stile. Cross it and enter the wood, following the footpath up a hill. At a cross-track keep going straight ahead, and at a waymarker turn right.

3. At the next track crossing, turn left. Follow this path along the ridge, with fine views to the left and right. As you reach a field, follow the path along the right-hand side until it descends into woodland. Leave the wood by a stile and

turn left, with a hedge on the left. At the far end keep straight on and go over a stile to enter a wood. Continue along the footpath, crossing over a stile into a field and following the path, with the wood on your right-hand side. It leads to a stile on the right and, after crossing it, to a path with a high wooden fence on the right. Go through a wooden gate and continue straight ahead as the path descends to a tarmac driveway. When the driveway meets Pitt Lane, continue ahead into Hammondswood Road.

4. Walk down Hammondswood Road, passing a house, St Austins, and then take the public footpath to the right. This leads to a wooden bridge crossing the River Wey. Follow the path until you reach the churchyard of St Mary's Church, Frensham. Walk through the churchyard, visit the church, and reach The Street. Turn left, then right into Lovers Lane. The public footpath continues to meet Bacon Lane. Turn left and then shortly right up a public footpath and onto the common. At a cross-tracks, turn right and at the next fork keep right, walking through an area of heather. The path drops down and, on reaching a sandy track, turn right and follow it back to the car park.

Where to eat and drink

In a wonderful setting overlooking Frensham Great Pond, the Frensham Pond Hotel provides refreshment for visitors. There is nothing better on a sunny day than to sit on their patio watching ducks on the water and enjoying a pleasant lunch. Alternatively, cups of tea and ice creams can be obtained from the visitor centre.

What to see

The Frensham Pond Visitor Centre has a good display about the natural history of Frensham Common and the Great Pond, and gives an insight into the variety of wildlife to be seen here. It also has a board listing all the bird species that have been seen recently on or around the Pond.

While you're there

Birdworld, in Farnham, has a splendid collection of birds from all over the world and takes part in several conservation projects. It is a fascinating place to visit for both young and old – it also has a small collection of farm animals and an interesting aquarium. The demonstrations featuring birds of prey are particularly impressive.

TAKING A WANDER AROUND FARNHAM

DISTANCE/TIME	4 miles (6.4km) / 2hrs
ASCENT/GRADIENT	374ft (114m) / ▲
PATHS	Paved streets and country park trails, can be muddy
LANDSCAPE	Attractive market town in informal parkland setting
SUGGESTED MAP	AA Walker's Map 23 Guildford, Farnham & The Downs
START/FINISH	Grid reference: SU837475
DOG FRIENDLINESS	Good in Farnham Park, poor in busy town centre
PARKING	Farnham Park, just off Castle Hill, Farnham
PUBLIC TOILETS	Farnham Park and The Hart, near Lower Hart car park

Farnham is a civilised little town with something to suit all tastes: boutique shops, plenty of culture in the shape of galleries and workshops, a plethora of places to eat and drink, and some gorgeous pockets of green space to relax in when you've tired of the busy streets. Farnham's most notable single feature is its grand old castle, which has presided over the town for more than 900 years.

Henry of Blois founded Farnham Castle in 1138, and it remained the official residence of the Bishops of Winchester until the Diocese of Guildford was created in 1927. Henry's successors strengthened the original castle by degrees, and added the Bishop's Palace at the foot of the 12th-century keep. One of its most famous residents was Cardinal Henry Beaufort, who presided at the trial of Joan of Arc in 1414. St Joan of Arc's Church in Farnham is dedicated to the French heroine. After the Civil War in 1648, more buildings were constructed in the castle's grounds, the most impressive being those built by Bishop George Morley, who spent more than £8,000 repairing the castle in the 17th century. You'll see glimpses of the castle from the park, and there are fantastic views of the town from the keep. The architecture reflects changing styles through the ages, which marks out Farnham Castle as one of the most important historical buildings in southern England. With the help of a Heritage Lottery Fund award, the Keep and Bishop's Palace have been completely renovated. Under the guardianship of English Heritage, the Keep re-opened to the public in July 2010. Join a guided tour and enjoy the superb exhibition detailing the 900 years of history of the castle; entrance is free.

The walk begins in Farnham Park, which was enclosed around 1376 as one of the two deer parks belonging to the Bishops of Winchester. Parliamentary troops were billeted here during the Civil War, and the Women's Land Army grew food crops in the park during World War II. Nowadays, you'll find playing fields, playgrounds and a public golf course, but most of the park is informal countryside, rich with wildlife and ripe for roaming.

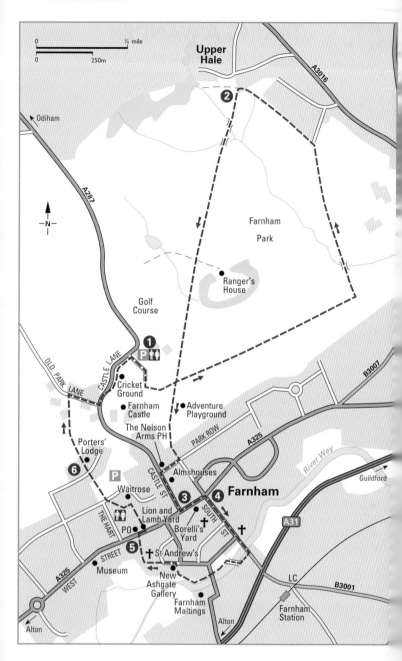

1. Bear right out of the very end of the car park, then bear left up the long avenue of trees to reach a tarmac path at the end of the avenue. Turn left onto this path, cross the brook, and continue under power lines to the information board near an entrance to the park. Continue on the same path, running behind houses, to the next park entrance.

2. Turn left onto another tarmac path that runs diagonally across the park, cross a bridge over a stream back under the power lines and past the Ranger's House. You'll cross the outward path within sight of the car park, before this path leads you out of the park along an alley, emerging on Park Row. Turn right here, then left into Castle Street. On your left you'll pass a row of brick almshouses, built in 1619 for the 'habitation and relief of eight poor honest old impotent persons'.

3. Continue to the bottom of Castle Street, where a flower market trades on the site where the old timber-framed market house stood from 1566 to 1866. Cross the road here (alternatively, continue left to the corner and cross with the lights), then turn left into The Borough and continue past Borelli's Yard.

4. At the corner, turn right into South Street, and continue ahead to cross Victoria Road, Union Road and then The Bridge Weyside in quick succession. Finally, cross the river, then turn right into Gostrey Meadow. The path leads across a wooden footbridge over the river before bearing left through the gardens. Cross the road and continue along the riverside, with Farnham Maltings across the water on your left. Bear right through the car park towards the New Ashgate Gallery, then turn left into Lower Church Lane. Continue left into St Andrew's churchyard, and follow the cobbled path past the west door and up the narrow lane with its signpost pointing towards the Museum of Farnham.

5. Emerge on West Street, opposite the post office. Cross at the lights, turn right and continue for 100yds (91m), then turn left through the arch into the Lion and Lamb Yard. At the top, you reach Waitrose; turn left under the colonnade, then bear right through Lower Hart car park to the exit. Turn left for a few steps, cross the road and turn left up Scholars Way, a paved path which leads between Farnham Baptist Church and the University for the Creative Arts. Continue past the Porters' Lodge, up the steps and out of the college campus.

6. Keep straight on up some rustic steps and straight across a field. In the next field, take the right-hand path along the edge of the field to a waymark post. Bear right down a narrow path that leads between fences and out onto Old Park Lane. Turn right, cross Castle Hill and walk up steps before turning left along the railed roadside footpath. Pass Farnham Cricket Club and turn right at the signposted entrance to Farnham Park and the car park.

Where to eat and drink

With over 40 pubs, restaurants and cafés in Farnham town centre, you won't go hungry. If you're looking for a pub, try the 450-year-old The Nelson Arms in Castle Street; there's a good choice of real ales, and also hot and cold food. A little further on you'll find a huge range of baguettes, as well as lunches and teas, at the licensed Lion and Lamb Café and Restaurant in Lion and Lamb Yard. At the beginning and end of your walk, the attractive Tenth Hole coffee shop is handy for hot and cold drinks, snacks and fantastic cakes and desserts.

TITLES IN THE SERIES

- 50 Walks in Berkshire & Buckinghamshire
- 50 Walks in the Brecon Beacons & South Wales
- 50 Walks in Cornwall
- 50 Walks in the Cotswolds
- 50 Walks in Derbyshire
- 50 Walks in Devon
- 50 Walks in Dorset
- 50 Walks in Durham & Northumberland
- 50 Walks in Essex
- 50 Walks in Gloucestershire
- 50 Walks in Hampshire & the Isle of Wight
- 50 Walks in Herefordshire & Worcestershire
- 50 Walks in Hertfordshire
- 50 Walks in Kent
- 50 Walks in the Lake District
- 50 Walks in London
- 50 Walks in Norfolk
- 50 Walks in North Yorkshire
- 50 Walks in Oxfordshire
- 50 Walks in the Peak District
- 50 Walks in Shropshire
- 50 Walks in Snowdonia & North Wales
- 50 Walks in Somerset
- 50 Walks in Staffordshire
- 50 Walks in Suffolk
- 50 Walks in Surrey
- 50 Walks in Sussex & the South Downs
- 50 Walks in Warwickshire & West Midlands
- 50 Walks in West Yorkshire
- 50 Walks in Wiltshire
- 50 Walks in the Yorkshire Dales